Form and Style
in
Indian English Fiction

Form and Style in Indian English Fiction

Edited by

JAGDISH BATRA

Prestige

an international publishing house

Published by

Prestige Books

New Delhi 110 058

Ph. 011-25507139

email: prestigebooks@gmail.com

website: asiabookclub.com

Associate Office

60/29-45 Parramatta Road,

Concord, NSW 2137

Australia

ISBN: 81-7851-087-1

Printed at Chaman Offset Press, New Delhi 110 002

Contents

Section III: Narratological Studies

Preface

It has been commonly observed that the thematic appreciation of a piece of literature is prioritized over its stylistic study. The theme of a creative work is certainly important because, with the proliferation of knowledge of human affairs, newer ideas appeal to the fancy of the writer, but the style too is equally important because of the mind-boggling advances made in this area in our times. We cannot simply afford to ignore this fast-expanding field. It is with this end in view that the present collection of articles related to stylistic and narratological studies of Indian fiction produced in English has been compiled.

Why Indian English Fiction?—the question might legitimately be asked. Experience shows that whereas style studies of English literature produced in the West are easy to come by, the situation is quite different in case of such studies of Indian English Literature. So, whereas Indian students get ample study-material along these lines on the western literature, there is acute dearth of good books on Indian literature. This is not a happy scenario considering the fact that of late, there has been a great profusion of Indian English novels. This book is, therefore, expected to contribute to the filling up of that vacuum in a modest manner. An attempt has been made to select articles covering Indian English novelists of bygone as well as contemporary times, viz., R.K. Narayan, Kamala Markandaya, Anita Desai, Rohinton Mistry, Jhumpa Lahiri, Arundhati Roy, Amitav Ghosh, Kiran Desai, Arvind Adiga et al.

At the risk of inviting allegations of reductionism, my write-up in the introductory part deals with the evolution of style into stylistics as also of simple plot structure into narratology. This, I must admit, is a layman's attempt at understanding the complex warp and woof of the subject. However, this is amply counterbalanced by the scholarly essay penned by Prof. Z.N. Patil, a well-known authority on stylistics in the country. In his inimitable style, he deals, among other things, with the poststructural phase of stylistics, lucidly elaborating the fine points. The articles that appear in the following pages conform broadly to the twofold division of stylistic and narratological analyses. Starting with traditional format, scholars go on to scrutinize selected Indian English novels on the basis of different structural and post-structural models.

I take this opportunity to thank the contributors, some of whom like Prof. S.L. Paul and Prof. Rekha Beniwal, responded to my request at a very short notice. I am greatly obliged to Prof. Alessandro Monti, Head of the Dept. of Oriental Studies at the University of Turin (Italy), for allowing the use of his erudite article which was published originally in his wonderful book *Society, Culture, Diaspora: A Reading of Indian Literature*. My sincere thanks to all the contributors who include my worthy fellow teachers as well as students. I shall be failing in my duty if I forget to acknowledge my gratitude to Prof. R.K. Dhawan of Delhi University, who has always inspired me in my academic pursuits. Also thanks to M/s Prestige Books for bringing out this book so very elegantly and expeditiously.

JAGDISH BATRA
(drjagdishbatra@rediffmail.com)

Stylistics and Narratology: An Overview

JAGDISH BATRA

The road from style to stylistics and from simple plot structure/ form to narratology is not so smooth. Beginning our journey, first into the territory of style, we find that the multiplicity of terms signifying different types of stylistics linked to different approaches and methodologies is sufficient indicator of the complexity involved in the study. Some of these terms are: Linguistic Stylistics, Pedagogical Stylistics, Functional Stylistics, Feminist Stylistics, Structural Stylistics, Cognitive Stylistics, Expressive Stylistics, Discourse Stylistics etc. It was perhaps, with this plurality in mind that the French linguist Jean-Jacques Lecercle observed: "No one has ever known exactly what the term stylistics comprises yet the subject is forever being reborn" (Wales 373). However, one must risk saying the unsayable, as Derrida would have it, to set the stage for the stylistic studies that appear in the following pages.

In order to appreciate the present state of style, stylistics and narratology, which is the focus of this book, it would be fruitful to remind ourselves of their basics and history. Simply put, the term 'style' refers to a certain mode of action or expression. Thus, a particular way of wearing clothes or of building a house, composing a piece of music or setting the dining table can be referred to as a particular style. In literature, by the term 'style,' we normally understand the manner of writing—the way in which words are arranged to convey what the writer wishes to convey to the reader. This depends on a number of factors like diction, prosody, syntax, sound patterns etc. The scope of style can be broadened to include imagery, metaphors, irony etc.

Style is the descendent of the rhetoric of yore. A rhetorician aimed at putting forth his views in a convincing manner so as to win over the court or the audience. For this, he depended upon rhetorical figures of speech or schemes which favoured using different patterns of words without bringing about any change in meaning, as for example, the use of anaphora, apostrophe, zeugma etc. These as well as the figures of thought or tropes like irony are therefore legitimate concerns of style. During Cicero's time, the principle of decorum decreed that the social class of the speaker and the occasion be kept in mind while deciding upon style. Over the period, based on different considerations, a number of classifications of style have emerged. Thus, we relate style to an individual, register, period, school, genre etc. to form distinctions like Shakespearean, legal, Elizabethan, Romantic and poetic respectively. A long chain of scholars has contributed to the critical understanding of style and narratology over the ages.

The Twentieth Century

The twentieth century saw a lot of development that had a bearing on our understanding of style. The most important influence which was to manifest itself much later—ironically due to the language barrier—in the form of a revolutionary breakthrough, was Ferdinand de Saussure's work *Cours de Linguistique Generale* (Course in General Linguistics) published in 1916. Saussure taught at the University of Geneva but the book was produced after his death by his pupils—Charles Bally and Albert Sechaye mainly, who put together their class notes along with those of some other class-mates, and immortalized the observations of their great master on the subject of linguistics. This work was widely read in French by scholars all over Europe before it was translated into English in 1959 for American students by Wade Baskin. Language as a subject had so far been studied diachronically in the form of philology before Saussure changed the approach to synchronic and came up with the notions of *signifier* and *signified* as parts of a sign. The signs were, he pointed out, related to each other in differential or oppositional manner. Within language, Saussure called the conventions and the system of language governing the utterance *langue* and the actual utterance *parole*. This insight into language was to form the basis of the epoch-making movement called structuralism which impacted not only literature but also many other disciplines.

Meanwhile, around the same time, the Russian Formalists, inspired by their predecessors and under the banner of The Formalist Linguistic Circle of Moscow, with which Roman Jakobson (1896-1982) was associated, rejected undue focus on the author in literary criticism and favoured an approach based upon analysis of the language of a text in relation to its psychological effect on the reader. Surprisingly, Charles Bally, Saussure's pupil, who was the first to use the term 'Stylistics' in his book *Traite de stylistique francaise* (1909), also defined it as the "study of the 'affective' elements in language—these affective elements being conceived as optional additions to an already determinate meaning" (Hough 6), which comes quite close to the Formalists' understanding of the subject. The Moscow group comprised linguists, literary critics and psychologists, who later developed the foregrounding theory. They opposed the Aristotelian mimetic theory and, in its place, favoured 'defamiliarisation' in literature because to them literature was just a linguistic product which had to be studied scientifically. The Russian Formalists were, in effect, the first stylisticians, but their work could not reach the western academies because of the 1917 Bolshevik Revolution that transformed Russia into the Soviet Union. The gulf that emerged between the western democracies and this newly-formed communist nation also impacted the academic domain. It was only in the 1960s, when Todorov translated some seminal texts into French that the West came to know of these tenets.

Roman Jakobson (1896-1982), a brilliant student of Moscow University, was a member of the Moscow Linguistic Circle and was associated with avant-garde art and poetry. He left Moscow in 1920, at the height of the Russian Revolution, and moved to Prague, to work on his doctoral thesis. Here, he became a member of the Prague Structuralist Circle. When Czechoslovakia also became a communist country, Jakobson moved over to America in 1941, carrying along with him the seeds of what was to become Stylistics later. The Prague group was also keenly interested in the linguistic structure of texts. Jan Mukarovsky, a member of this group, laid stress on the 'literariness' of text, i.e., the special use of language in a literary work which tended to 'foreground' the utterance. Victor Shklovsky, another formalist, termed this use of language as 'defamiliarizing' what was commonly observed but then this property was explained differently from the way the Romantic critic Coleridge did. According to the revised notion, it is not the author who brings about defamiliarization, rather it is the language that performs the trick. Roman Jakobson identified these 'deviations' in phonological and grammatical constructions as also in versification and imagery.

The work of the Russian Formalists belongs to the period of the 1920s, but as submitted earlier, due to the political turmoil engulfing the communist countries, the findings of the Russian formalists took time to reach the democratic society of the West. In the meantime, the critics I.A. Richards and William Empson had also been concentrating on the literary texts as also on the way readers were affected by those texts. This approach was called Practical Criticism—a term taken from Richards' book *Practical Criticism* (1929)—which gained ground in England of the 1930s. This approach, as also the literary essays of T.S. Eliot (*Selected Essays* 1932), inspired a new movement in the U.S.A. called New Criticism—a term made popular by John Crowe Ransom's book *The New Criticism* (1941). Other advocates of this approach included Cleanth Brooks, René Wellek, R.P. Blackmur, Allen Tate and William K. Wimsatt. The New Criticism was based almost exclusively on the close study of literary works as independent aesthetic objects, but Practical Criticism tended to pay more attention to the psychological aspects involved in the reader's interaction with the text. Both schools, i.e., the Russian Formalists and the New Critics decried the prevalent tendency to delve deep into the biographies of writers while assessing their work. Later, the American New Critics also focussed on features like irony, paradox and metaphor, but they did not apply the science of linguistics to poetry as the Russian Formalists did.

Linguistic Stylistics

Consequently, the traditional notion of style was replaced by what has come to be known as 'stylistics,' meaning the science of style. It shows the growing impact of science which insisted on an objective study of literature, denying to it any mystique. Some of the works which laid down the roadmap for stylistics in Anglo-American criticism were Leo Spitzer's *Stilstudeien* (1928) and *Linguistics and Literary History* (1948), Thomas Sebeok's anthology titled *Style in Language* (1960), in which Roman Jakobson's article titled 'Closing Statement: Linguistics and Poetics' appeared, Roger Fowler's edited work *Essays on Style in Language* (1966) and Geoffrey Leech's *A Linguistic Guide to English Poetry* (1969). The grammarian Bloomfield's article 'Linguistic Aspects of Science' is also considered an important milestone in the importation of scientism in language study.

The increased interest in linguistics is what distinguishes linguistic stylistics, also referred to as applied linguistics or simply as stylistics. In order to correct the bias in impressionistic analysis of texts, it undertakes the examination of lexis, grammar, syntax, phonological properties and discursive devices and leaves theme, character and environment of the text out. Stylistics has already re-defined some of the conventional features, as for example, alliteration, which is now called phonological parallelism. Apart from them, grammatical parallelism and deviation of language use from the normal one are considered foregrounding of language over literary features.

The increased focus on linguistic and stylistic categories pertaining to lexical, phonological and syntactical choices has the inherent danger of getting reduced to obsession with statistical data. In this regard, one cannot avoid mentioning Enkvist's formulation which is almost a mathematical model. He defines the linguistic aspect of stylistics as "the function of the aggregate of the ratios between the frequencies of its phonological, grammatical and lexical items and the frequencies of the corresponding items in a contextually related norm." No wonder then that in their search for an out-and-out objective evaluation of literature, the stylisticians have also turned to computers to count different linguistic/grammatical elements. This method is called stylometry.

This kind of stylistic examination, then, yields statistical figures that require careful interpretation even though some scholars believe that the meaning pre-exists in the language and it requires no further interpretation. According to Herbert Read, short sentences convey an impression of speed and therefore are suited to the description of action. Similarly, long sentences are indicative of deliberation and solemnity. The complex sentences suit complex ideas and feeling and anticipatory constituents in a sentence bring in an element of suspense. Fowler points out that tag questions are demanding and pointedly request confirmation of an assertion made already. Again, rhetorical questions, according to Quirk and Greenbaum, function as forceful statements, which of course, is nothing new since rhetoric has always been studied as the art of persuasive oratory.

Limitations

Close reading for the sake of linguistic/stylistic analysis may be applied to a novel just as it is done in the case of a poem, but then one cannot hope to put the entire bulk of a novel through this mechanism, without boring the reader to death and the critic himself to lunacy. One could select at random one or more passages and submit them to close reading. But the representative part of a novel has to be selected carefully "not seeing the wood for the oaks, or the larches for the chestnuts" (Lodge 79). Also, "The features which recommend themselves to the attention in one text will not necessarily be important in another text by the same or a different author" (Leech 74). There is, thus, no guarantee of uniformity in such matters. Moreover, the critic has to compare it with a text which he considers to be the standard. Now, scholars are not unanimous in considering a text as a standard. Such an exercise does not discount the value of inspiration or intuition. When a critic chooses an element, a specimen of deviation, for analysis, the effort primarily is about a meaningful word or passage. Spitzer calls it 'click.' There is every possibility that another critic would select a different set of *lexis* and explain according to his whims, insight and intuition.

One wonders what purpose is served through painstaking search for the number and class of nouns, adjectives, verbs, adverbs or number of words in a sentence. Leech and Short, who take great pains in detailing all the style markers, also point out the limitations: "There is no direct relation between statistical deviance and stylistic significance: literary considerations must therefore guide us in selecting what features to examine" (70). If, after counting a certain category of words, we say that the writer X has so many of them per page while the writer Y has these many, it does mark the writer out in one way and this fact could be used to point out the stylistic signature of a writer. But then a writer grows and the style changes: "Received ideas about the style of a particular period or a particular author sometimes turn out to have no basis in fact when subjected to this kind of investigation" (Hough 54). Then, whereas the literary critic undertakes to combine analysis with variable evaluation, the stylistician relies on a technical scale of value or simply puts it aside.

The American structuralists felt perturbed that their efforts were liable to be frustrated if they allowed the considerations of meaning to influence their analysis, since semantic intuition did not seem to be amenable to objective control. But if a linguist aims at saying something really worthwhile about a literary text, he can ill-afford to ignore meaning otherwise he would only provide justification for critics like G.D. Martin who assert that "linguists bring us to the threshold of meaning and then bid us farewell" (26). Keeping in view these difficulties, Freeman came up with the novel suggestion that a linguist should analyze the text and then pass on the results of his analysis to a literary critic for the purpose of interpretation. (Chhibber 178)

Concluding this short discussion on the subject, it can be said that effective style analysis may or may not demand a rigorous stylistic or statistical examination. Such a thing might help in understanding a work that is linguistically complex; it may not be needed where the language follows normal conventions. The organizing aesthetic principle of a work will also decide the methodology that ought to be adopted by the critic. Intuition will never be redundant. Peter Verdock has rightly commented that the stylistic approach "exemplifies a perspective, namely a perspective on the study of literature, and [. . .] it should be emphasized that it is not the only one, nor is it distinct from all others" (55).

Scope Extended

The entire gamut of structuralism is based upon this twin-layered notion of sign, propounded mainly by Saussure. Literature was viewed as an artifact of language. A poem was a structure consisting of different units like words, sounds, punctuation etc. The structuralist critics applied linguistic concepts to literary text, as for example, the distinction between phonemic and morphemic levels of organization which meant the text was self-referential. The aim of the structuralist criticism was not to interpret individual texts, but to unveil the grammar embedded in a literary work which governed its form and meaning. Through the identification of this grammar, they hoped to underline how meaning is produced.

With the dawn of post-structuralism, the literary work was re-defined as a text whose author was declared dead by Roland Barthes. The textuality, by extension, lost its distinction as purely literary outpouring and became "writing-in-general" (Abrams 241). When Jacques Derrida, the high priest of post-structuralism waved the wand of deconstruction, he changed the old fixity of meaning into an illusory trace—deferred and different forever and locked within the domain of language.

However, Michel Foucault's notion of discourse changed the critical perspective again and brought milieu into the picture. Discourse connected text with context. So, stylistics now had two broad categories, as Bradford puts it: textualist and contextualist. Whereas the textualist stylisticians focus on prosody, metaphors, syntax, vocabulary etc., the contextualists seek contexts in which reader's competence and socio-cultural forces affect systems of signification. Context is not mere physical circumstances but also the values, beliefs and ideas of the people living at a particular time in a particular society. Meaning and knowledge are no longer believed to pre-exist the text in the language itself. It may however be pointed out that the reader now has his subject position entirely as a product of social forces and practices. The literary phenomenon is viewed as a dialectic between such a reader and the text in which the meaning is generated.

The poststructuralist scenario, thus, is marked by attention to semantics alongside semiotics. It has been felt that the meanings derived from particular usage have become mechanistic and the context is being totally overlooked. Even the text, when it forms the immediate context of a passage selected for stylistic analysis, was relegated to background, disrupting the organic unity of the text. By underlining the importance of context, the overmuch stress on the linguistic aspect is sought to be balanced.

The concern with sociolinguistic aspects creates the stylistic genre called discourse analysis which has been in vogue since the 1970s. Discourse denotes all literary and non-literary verbal (spoken or written) construction or production in the linguistic mode. In this kind of analysis, language is taken as a living form that involves the speaker or writer addressing the hearer or the reader respectively. It also takes into account the situation and the socio-cultural conventions prevalent in a society at a particular point of time. It is based on the premise that both the speaker and the listener are aware of the linguistic code and the attendant connotational aspects so that the meaning becomes clear. "If an utterance seems purposely to violate these expectations, we seek to make sense of it by transferring it to a context in which it is clearly appropriate" (Abrams 77).

This is a view that is opposed to that of the deconstructionists who viewed language as detached from history and discourse without centre. In one respect however, a section of the discourse analysts on the one hand and the deconstructionists on the other seem to agree and that is the belief that language alone cannot express what the writer wishes to convey through it. The reservation of the deconstructionists has already been mentioned; some discourse analysts feel that the surface meaning of a text is only a rouge used to cover what the writer could not say. Similarly, the gaps in a text are supposed to contain meaning.

The Foucauldian model of analysis called Critical Discourse Analysis takes into consideration the nature of discourse, which is defined as a set of relationships existing in society as a result of the power structure. This engagement of discourse with the power structure manifests itself in the form of rules, norms, social conventions and institutions. Incessant power struggle is a reality according to Foucault and it has a bearing on the existing structure and discursive formations.

The pragmatists among the structuralists, who were upset over excessive stress on theory, felt that not much attention had been paid to the unwritten code of conduct that attends upon verbal exchanges or discourse in society. Therefore, the notions of politeness, compliments, euphemism etc. and the imperatives of speech-act theory had to be taken into account. "Pragmatics is concerned with the meaning of language in discourse, that is, when it is used in an appropriate context to achieve particular aims. Pragmatic meaning is not, we should note, an alternative to semantic meaning, but complementary to it, because it is inferred from the interplay of semantic meaning with context" (Verdock 19). In fact, the pragmatists felt that despite their seeming avoidance of interpretation, what most theories have achieved is to have given rise to newer interpretations. This stand goes counter to the concept of fallacy of authorial intention postulated by Wimsatt and Beardsley. To the pragmatists, there can be no meaning without intention. Pragmatics, therefore, engages with sociolinguistics and communication approaches and in this way shifts the focus on to the reader and the situation.

Another newly-developed genre labelled 'Social Semiotics' looks upon language as a function of social and cultural forces at work at a particular point of time in society. It looks at the ways in which different aspects of modern society combine to create meaning. The 'semiotic resources' surrounding us include obvious modes of communication such as language, gesture, images and music, as also the less obvious ones like food, dress and everyday objects, all of which carry cultural value and significance Practical exercises and examples as wide ranging as furniture arrangements in public places, advertising jingles, photojournalism etc. provide readers with the knowledge and skills they need to analyse and also produce successful multi-model texts and designs.

This extension of stylistics has been justified as it seeks to find causal relationship between the stylistic character of literary texts and their social and ideological contexts. There seem minor differences between different approaches like those of the pragmatists, discourse analysts, sociolinguists etc. but all of them are joined at the roots to culture. In addition to literature as we have known it, 'media-discourses' such as films, advertising, news reports, songs and political speeches have also been brought within the scope of stylistics. What is important to note here is that none of the text types gets precedence over any other.

Having said that, it must also be pointed out that the focus of the contemporary stylistics is linguistic criticism and not literary criticism. Sometimes, the distinction between the two gets blurred. For example, the approach of what has come to be known as Feminist Stylistics which underlines the male prejudice against female as found in the use of language is appreciable but feminist criticism of any type, it is finally revealed, is anchored to ideological grounds. Under the circumstances, Feminist Stylistics becomes a handmaiden to the ideology of feminism.

II

Narratology

In the case of fiction, the stylistic examination beyond the length of a sentence takes us into the domain of narratology, which can be defined as the style of narrating a story. There is no doubt that the story element has formed the kernel of literature on the whole, even as the notion of narrative is now sought to be applied to a wide range of disciplines. The ancient literature in the form of epic or drama thrives on narrative although the manner of narration is different. Aristotle analyzed the ancient Greek drama and identified the beginning, middle and end of a play as worthy of attention by the dramatist. He also identified the elements of hamartia, peripetia, anagnorisis etc., which were and are even now considered vital to the development of character and action in the drama.

Since its origin in the eighteenth century, the novel has steadily risen in popularity. It occupies in contemporary times a position that can very well be compared to that of the drama in Elizabethan England. Narrative, being seminal to the novel, has therefore come to occupy a very important place and narratology, as the science of narrative, has become an important subject of critical study now. It may also be recalled that apart from the novel, short story and narrative poetry also need the story element. The twentieth century has seen the topsy-turveying of Victorian and Edwardian conventions. As in the case of stylistics, in narratology also, one encounters a plethora of terms linked to technique or theme, as for example, Structural Narratology, Cognitive Narratology, Visual Narratology, Natural Narratology, Confessional Narratology, Eco-Narratology, Feminist Narratology etc. The Russian Formalists, followed by the French structuralists, have contributed a lot to the study of narratives.

While dealing with the basics of a fictional account, we realize that the actual story is amorphous and it has to be refined into a plot. Only then the reader will feel interested in it. To the Russian Formalists, a *fabula* has to be turned into a *sjuzet*. The time in a plot could be stretched or amputated, depending upon the requirement of the story. It is virtually not possible to present on stage or in the pages of a novel all that happened in the life of different characters. We are interested in selective action that is relevant to the main interest or the theme of the text. In this respect, Seymour Chatman's five-fold division of time makes an interesting study: the *summary* abridges the time, while *ellipses* simply effaces time between the chapters or acts. In *scene*, the story time and the narrative time are the same, but in *stretch*, the time is stretched so that the reader/viewer can absorb the intricacy of a situation. In the fifth category of *pause*, the story simply stops, as for example, when the author describes the scene or the objects and action takes a back-seat for a while.

Broadly speaking, the story/ plot classification, as amended by the twentieth century studies can be comprehended by the three-fold division based on 'story' (the actual order and timing of events), 'text' (the portrayal of events in the literary work) and 'narration' (the manner of telling). These three divisions are referred to as *historie, recit* and *narration* by Gerard Genette. Another French scholar Roland Barthes' classification of *catalytic/ indexical*, corresponding to Chatman's *kernels/satellites* categories, refers to the events contributing to the furtherance of the narrative and the attending details like scenic or atmospheric description respectively.

Long before the Western linguists arrived on the scene, the Russian scholar Vladimir Propp's study of numerous folklores and their categorization in his *Morphology of the Folk Tale* (1928, trans. 1970) became an epoch-making event. He zeroed in on seven 'spheres of action' and thirty-one fixed 'functions' of narrative. On the other hand, the French anthropologist Claude Levi-Strauss took up myths and found that in thousands of them, the narratives contained some basic thematic structures. His notion of *mythemes* is modelled upon Saussure's phonemes. What he discovered was that like the self-referentiality of the linguistic signs, the myths seemed to relate to one another, rather than to reality. A.J. Greimas reduced this pattern further to certain binaries which included six *actants* or roles. These were—subject/object to account for the basic patterns of desire, aim or search; sender/receiver for conveying messages etc., and helper/opponent for auxiliary actions.

Instead of the inductive method of studying various narratives and then laying down the common points as Propp had done, Roland Barthes used the deductive method by breaking up Balzac's *Sarassine* into 561 segments in his book *S/Z*. He brought in linguistic elements and exploited their semantic worth to analyse a narrative just as he would a sentence, but such an approach, called *explication de texte*, providing for a long commentary—much more elaborate than the target text—could find few followers. (Sturrock 118). Mikhail Bakhtin, another compatriot of Propp, believed language to be basically dialogic because language made sense only in communication. He, therefore, focussed on parole rather than langue. His concepts of the carnival and polyphony in fiction are much respected even now.

As with the narrative, the narrator has also been classified by Gerard Genette into categories like *autodiegetic*, in which the narrator as the main protagonist relates the story in first person, as in Kamla Markandaya's *Nectar in a Sieve*; *homodiegetic* in which the narrator is not the leading character in the narrative and is mainly used to report the events as in the case of the village woman in Raja Rao's *Kanthapura*; and *heterodiegetic* in which the narrator is the omniscient author who is outside the narrative and tells the story in third person, as is the norm in most traditional novels. In contemporary novels, it is not uncommon to find a mélange of different types of narration in one text. Apart from these, the point of view becomes an important issue in the narrative and so is the notion of focalization. The narrative mode can be direct, indirect, or Free Indirect Discourse.

Closely allied to this mode is the technique of Stream of Consciousness. The term has been in vogue since the 1920s, when the psychologist William James used it to describe the unbroken flow of conscious and unconscious thoughts, feelings, perceptions, memories etc. While the writer's rendering of the thought processes of characters bears the tell-tale signs of the author's hand in Stream of Consciousness, the Interior Monologue is free from it. In his sincere effort to portray the goings-on in the human mind, the author has been faulted for dressing up in language the perceptions, thoughts, feelings etc. which may have existed at the pre-language level. In his unique work *The Life and Opinions of Tristram Shandy, Gentlemen*, the eighteenth-century pioneer of the genre of novel Laurence Sterne had resolved this point by presenting on the pages of his novel, paintings or dots and dashes or nothing at all to represent various states of mind. However, in contemporary fiction, the writers prefer to convert the non-verbal segments into verbal ones.

The Poststructural Phase

Narratology began basically as a formalist/structuralist enterprise. It was not supposed to help in exploring the relationship between the text and the author or between the text and the social context. In the poststructural phase, however, the semantic considerations have come to the fore, even as Jacques Derrida underlined the evanescent nature of meaning as the eternally deferred and differing 'trace.' His deconstructive mode of reading combines this linguistic insight with the identification of any logical vulnerability of the text—a thematic aspect—to arrive at the indeterminacy of meaning.

The other poststructuralist way of approaching the meaning is to refer to social reality. The text is the site for the negotiation of meaning and discourse connects the text to the context. If the writing has been deconstructed in this manner, so has the reader or the subject been. We understand the subject today as a construction effected by different discourses. Analysis of text has thus become the analysis of intertextualities and dialogic histories. And yet the distinction between a thematic examination and a narratological one does exist.

As in case of stylistic analysis, a caveat needs to be entered in respect of narratology also and it is that while undertaking the narratological study of a narrative, as for example a gender-narrative or any type of postcolonial narrative, the critic is tempted to make a foray into the ideological field even though, ideally speaking, narratology should be concerned with the working out of different narratological elements or schema or 'grammar' only. This is because what we have in mind is the idea of narrative as a mode of representation of social reality and a writer has his or her own perception of it which can be called his ideology. Perfect severance of content from thought is well-nigh impossible. But the chief focus of study has to be the *way* in which the object of the writer has been achieved—the *how* rather than the *what*. The aim of narratology is to characterize narrative 'langue.'

Elaborating this point, we can take up the example of spatial reading which according to Mickleson is "a mode of narrative structure that foregrounds thematic rather than chronological or causal principle of order" (556). Spatial reading is particularly favoured while discussing the space available to the hitherto oppressed classes like women, transgenders, handicapped and the economically depressed segments of population—both individually and collectively. Similarly, in case of eco-narratives, the term 'space' is used in a more concrete, literal sense. Now, while studying the narratological dimensions, it becomes quite problematic to refrain from an examination of ideological commitment of the author. Still, the chief focus of the narratologist should be to focus on the way in which the concept of space shapes the narrative.

This kind of approach in which a thematic idea shapes the narrative is studied in two ways: as Thematology uses paradigmatic approach, i.e., it traces the evolution of a thematic model through the history of ideas—how it has been handled in the past and what changes have occurred in its use over a period of time. It deals with the three poles of subject matter or complete plot, theme or idea and smaller motifs which are the building blocks of the narrative. Motifs may denote any kind of content like a character, situation, object or an abstract quality. The other option of Narrative Thematics is also a thematic approach based on formalism. A narrative is broken into motifs to understand the narrative structure. However, not every motif need be of importance to the causal growth of a narrative. Naturally, semantic considerations play their part here, for the interaction of characters and motif-configurations gives rise to abstract meanings. In fact, theme has always been important for the shaping of a narrative. The function of narratology here is to study how the theme shapes a narrative by unifying its paradoxes and ambiguities, digressions and silences.

In these postmodern times, newer concepts continue to turn heads. Theoreticians like Roland Barthes, Claude Bremond and Francois Lyotard have freed narrative from fiction and even literature. "No sooner had narrative come of age as a theoretical concept than it began to invade fields as diverse as historiography, medicine, law, psycho-analysis, and ethnography" (Ryan 344). Therefore, the term 'narrative of the science' is as acceptable to postmodern man as the 'narrative of history.' At the root of this chaos lies the feeling that what was known as reality to our ancestors is now a 'narrative,' a fictitious one at that, which would not exclude even science because the latter "does not discover truths but fabricates them according to the rules of its own game in a process disturbingly comparable to the overt working of narrative fiction" (*ibid*).

The emergence of technocriticism, in sync with the present revolution in information technology has added a new dimension to our thinking about text and its reception by the reader. The text or the hyper-text in the digital domain is, truly speaking, a network of texts. The search engines are helpful in locating different texts centring on the same *lexia* (unit) to which a surfer returns again and again. What this type of reading gives to the reader is the reconfiguration of the text. The narrative is no longer closed or linear; rather it is open, non-linear and non-hierarchical, since all links have similar pathways and presentations. The reader also has the liberty to create his own narrative on numerous sites in this virtual world. The text can be re-arranged, deleted or added to at the flick of a button. These facilities have given rise to the practice of cumulative writing of literary texts through networking and virtual chains. It is an exciting field of creativity and criticism which is fast changing our understanding of literature. But instant creativity through this mode also means brief life-span of the virtual text. This kind of mass participation in literary and critical effort makes literature and criticism popular but brings in the attendant problem of blurring of distinction between good and bad. That, however, seems the *fait accompli* in these postmodern times.

III

Indian Poetics and Fiction

The Indian view of style and stylistics also needs to be noted here, since in these postmodern times, hierarchies are demolished and no concept is treated as marginal. The Indian notion of *reeti* deals with the linguistic style. Around ninth century A.D., Acharya Vaaman is deemed to have expounded it for the first time but even before him, Banabhatta, Bhamah and Dandi had expostulated different stylistic formats. Even though some distinctions like *Vaidarbhi*, *Gaudi* and *Panchali* are named after different regions or provinces, these are related to linguistic use, as a critic avers: "Actually, there is no impact of the geographical entity referred to as province here. Vaaman believes that the *reetis* existed in seed-form before the provinces were named" (Vedalankar 131; my trans.). This division is similar to the notion of grand, middle or plain styles created by the classical rhetoricians of the Western literature. Apart from it, the concept of *vakrokti* (literally 'crooked statement') in Hindi literature, as enunciated by Kuntak, can be compared to 'deviance.' *Vakrokti* is an umbrella term which covers a number of stylistic, semantic and thematic distinctions. Out of the six classifications of *vakrokti*, three belong to the linguistic framework and refer to elements of deviation like phonological parallelism and amalgamation of registers, figures of speech like humanization and objectification, word selection and mutation etc. The other forms covered by the term address wit and irony and changes wrought in narrative to heighten a particular *rasa* or aesthetic pleasure.

According to the noted critic Nagendra, "There is a strange affinity between the Western poetics and the Indian poetics, not only with regard to fundamental principles, but also in their various manifestations. This is particularly the case with the Indian *reeti* and the Western stylistics. [. . .] It goes without saying that this similarity does not indicate mutual contact or influence—this indicator of the basic unity of human thought was, by and large, a chance occurrence" (71; my trans.). The difference, however, lies in that the Indian linguists emphasize the human element also alongside the textual one.

The poststructuralist ethos of negating any hierarchy should also re-direct our attention to the indigenous concepts having a bearing on narratology. The overarching concepts of *rasa, dhvani* and *auchitya*, propounded by Bharatmuni, Anandvardhan and Kshemendra respectively play a vital role here also as these do in stylistics. Acharya Dhananjay in his work entitled *Dasha-rupa*, identifies five stages of action: beginning, endeavour (to achieve object), anticipation, certainty, and achievement or the lack of it. He also mentions five *sandhis* or junctures to indicate transitional stages. These then, define the narrative structure, but these are further related to different *rasas* or types of literary / artistic pleasure. Bharatmuni of the *Natyashastra* had defined eight main variants of *rasa*, viz., the valorous (*veer*), the furious (*raudra*), the terrible (*bhayanak*), the pathetic (*karun*), the erotic (*sringaar*), the comic (*haasya*), the disgusting (*veebhatsa*), and the fantastic (*adbhut*). The ninth *rasa*, viz., *shaant* or 'the peaceful' was added by Abhinavagupta. This *rasa* comes in the final stage of the plot when all action is supposed to resolve into peace, which is, according to the Indian philosophy, the highest goal of all human endeavour.

Apart from the *Rasa* theory, the *Dhvani* theory is also an important part of the Indian poetics. Whereas the former is an affective theory, the latter is based on semantics and was enunciated by Abhinavagupta. *Dhvani* suggests a special, transcendental meaning suggested by a word. Meaning exists at three levels in a word: *abhidha, lakshana* and *vyanjana*. *Abhidha* is the literal meaning of the expression and *lakshana* points to the affinity between signified and signifier in form. When these two levels do not lead the reader to the meaning which lies at a still deeper level, the *vyanjana* power of the word comes to his rescue. Indian grammarians have also laid down the sequence of the process of gathering meaning: from sound to word, and from word to a revelatory stage called *sphota* and from there to the meaning. The importance of the *Dhvani* theory can be gauged from the viewpoint of the aestheticians Anandavardhana and Abhinavagupta that the language of poetry, in crossing the realms of both *abhidha* and *lakshana*, crosses the bounds of empiricism. The ultimate aim of the poetic experience is peace or the *shaant rasa*. Leelavathy means much the same when she states, "No literary work that gives spiritual peace which Indians have described as 'samyoga visraanti' which Aristotle has described as

Catharsis a purging of heat and which Richards has described as equilibrium of mental state will debase man" (Tharakan 117).

From an early stage, motivated by the western penchant for verisimilitude in literature, the Indian English writers took to linguistic realism in a big way. So far as Indian poetics is concerned, "The ancient literary tradition, as embodied in the classical Sanskrit was dominated by classical theories of aesthetics and as such hardly ever recognized local colour or linguistic realism as a valid stylistic experiment" (Dey 42). Thus, in the changed scenario, taking a cue from the western practice, the Indian novelists successfully used strategies to achieve the realistic effect.

In this regard, the efforts of Mulk Raj Anand to Indianize English are widely recognized. His translation as well as transliteration of native words including swear-words, mis-spelling of English words, use of hybridization, duplicatives etc. have beautifully evoked the local colour. What Anand did selectively to words, Raja Rao, the other member of the great early trio of Indian English literature, did to the entire narrative of his novel *Kanthapura* and in this way imbued it with the local colour. Through a garrulous protagonist—an old rustic woman—Rao makes superb use of the rhythmic oral tradition, complete with digressions.

Anand's example has been followed by a large number of Indian English novelists. Some landmarks in the field of deft use of stylistic and narratological choices have come from writers—and this list is not at all exhaustive—like G.V. Desani known for his verbal pyrotechnics, Anita Desai for her poetic prose, Arundhati Roy for her neo-nativization of English, Salman Rushdie for his 'chutnification' of language, Vikram Seth for his use of verse in fiction and Kiran Desai for her stylistic flourishes. Besides, some other equally capable novelists who deserve mention are: Shashi Deshpande for using epistolary style, Amitav Ghosh for the skilful focalization of the narrator's point of view, Rohinton Mistry for richness of language and imagery et al. There are many more who have not attained prominence equal to the aforesaid novelists, but who have tried their hand at stylistic innovation, as for example, Amit Chaudhuri who almost dispenses with the narrative in a novel without depending on the stream of consciousness either, I. Allan Sealy for producing a linguistic period piece in an avowedly indigenous *nama* style, and Upamanyu Chatterjee for his use of pompous diction and Latinized construction.

There is no denying the fact that there has been tremendous amount of research in the twin fields of stylistics and narratology in the West to which the Indian corpus on the subject does not stand comparison but what has been outlined by the Indian thinkers has a permanent value even though the literary forms undergo changes with the passage of time. Now, whereas the studies of Indian English literature on the basis of Indian poetics are very few in number, those of the western literature are practically non-existent. The ancient Indian wisdom in this regard has yet to gain recognition.

In conclusion, it may be said with regard to style and narratology that the tribe is ever on the increase. A cursory glance at each new edition of any dictionary of stylistics or narratology would prove the point. It may be admitted that the segregation of style from content is easier said than done. The several meeting points between thematic and the stylistic / narratological aspects of a literary text support the postmodern scepticism of distinctions. Knowledge is, after all, one indivisible whole and it is for the sake of convenience that we indulge in categorization and classification.

Works Cited

Abrams, M.H. *A Handbook of Literary Terms*. New Delhi: Cengage Learning, 2009.

Bradford, Richard. *Stylistics. (The New Critical Idiom)* London: Routledge, 1997.

Chhibber, S.D.S. *Poetic Discourse: An Introduction to Stylistic Analysis*. New Delhi: Sterling, 1987.

Cuddon, J.A. *A Dictionary of Literary Terms and Literary Theory*. New Delhi: Maya Blackwell, 1998.

Dey, Esha. *The Novels of Raja Rao*. New Delhi: Prestige, 1992.

Enkvist, N.E. *Linguistic Stylistics*. New York: Walter De Gruyter, 1973.

Fowler, Roger, ed. *Essays on Style and Language*. London: University College, 1967.

Hough, Graham. *Style and Stylistics*. New York: Routledge & Kegan Paul, 1969.

Kachru, B.B. *The Indianization of English*. Madras: OUP, 1983.

Leech, Geoffrey N. & Short, Michael H. *Style in Fiction*. London: Longman, 1981.

Lodge, David, *Language in Fiction*. New York: Columbia University Press, 1967.

Martin, G.D. *Language, Truth and Poetry*. Edinburgh: Edinburgh University Press, 1975.

Mickleson, David J. "Spatial Form." *Routledge Encyclopedia of Narrative Theory*. Oxfordshire: Routledge, 2005. Indian Reprint 2008.

Nagendra, Dr. *Bharatiya Kavyashastra ki Bhumika*. Delhi: National, 1963.

Naik, M.K. & Shyamala A. Narayan. *Indian English Literature (1980-2000): A Critical Survey*. Delhi: Pencraft, 2007.

Patil, Z.N. *Indian English Fiction: A Stylistic Approach*. New Delhi: Prestige, 2008.

Pyrhonen, Heta. "Thematic Approaches to Narrative." *Routledge Encyclopedia of Narrative Theory*. Oxfordshire: Routledge, 2005. Indian Reprint 2008.

Quirk, R. and Greenbaum, S. *A University Grammar of English*. London: Longman, 1973. .

Read, Herbert. *English Prose Style*. Ludhiana: Lyall, 1968.

Ryan, Marie-Laure. 'Narrative' *Routledge Encyclopedia of Narrative Theory*. Oxfordshire: Routledge, 2005. Indian Reprint 2008.

Sturrock, John. *Structuralism* (Second edition). Oxford, UK: Blackwell, 2003.

Tharakan, K.M. *Western and Eastern Poetics*. London: Sangam, 1999.

Vedalankar, Vijay Kumar. *Kavyashastra Nirupan*. Delhi: Atlantic, 2009.

Verdock, Peter. *Stylistics*. London: Oxford University Press, 2002.

Wales, Katie. *A Dictionary of Stylistics*. Essex: Pearson, 2001.

Wellek, Rene & Warren Austin. *Theory of Literature*. Middlesex, UK: Penguin, 1993.

Stylistics and Appreciation of Indian English Fiction

Z.N. PATIL

There are various approaches to the study of literature. Let me put the proposition a bit more precisely. We can study it from autobiographical, sociological, psychological and historical, textual perspectives. We can study it in the light of structuralism, post-structuralism, deconstruction, postmodernism, psychoanalysis, feminism, lesbian feminism, gay criticism, Marxism, new historicism, cultural materialism, postcolonial criticism, narratology, and stylistics. These perspectives can be broadly classified into two major approaches- thematic and linguistic. But let me state at the outset that I do not subscribe to the fallacious dichotomy between form and content, manner and matter, and style and subject. In my opinion, any attempt to compartmentalize theme and language is a futile exercise. However, this does not in any way imply that we cannot discuss the two separately. But, while doing so, we have to refer to the other in order to make our discussion worthwhile, because the two are essentially inseparable, woven together or are mutually inclusive. Let me use an analogy from performing arts. Let us say that we are watching a dance performance by a seasoned dancer. When we are watching the performance, can we separate the dance from the dancer? Obviously, the answer is in the negative.

Role of Stylistics

The aim of the present paper is to talk about the application of stylistics to the study of literature. Stylistics plays a very significant role in the interpretation and appreciation of literature.

Stylistics uses the methods and findings of linguistics to analyze literary texts. Stylistics uses hard data to support intuitions about literary works. It suggests new interpretations of literary texts on the basis of linguistic evidence. It explains how literary meanings are made. Stylistics can be very fruitfully used to sensitize students to the beautiful aspects of literary expression. The linguistic aspect of literature is very significant. Alexander Pope is absolutely right when he says "what oft was thought, but never so well-expressed." Let me explain the point with an illustration. The teacher can demonstrate to the students how, for example, the different stanzas of Wordsworth's "The Solitary Reaper" are organized. He can draw the attention of the students to the fact that the poet highlights the solitariness of the reaper through the use of words and phrases such as 'solitary,' 'alone,' 'single' and 'by herself.' This awareness will give the students a feel of how synonymous expressions can be used to emphasize a point. This sort of exercise can be administered at school level. However, at an advanced level, teachers can use poetry to enrich the students' language. Once students have mastered the drab basics of English, teachers can acquaint them with the nuances of the language and bring to their notice how unusual, unique, uncommon, deviant or marked expressions can inject freshness into the language and enable them to view the world around them from a new perspective. However, it is not enough to explain how the deviant language is different from the routine language. The teacher has to go beyond this and explain why the poet, for instance, has used this special type of language.

In the present paper I would like to elaborate on three major approaches in stylistics: the text-linguistic approach, discourse approach and linguistic-functional nativization approach with the major focus on the last approach.

Text-Linguistic Approach

The emphasis of the present paper is on the analysis of linguistic rather than experiential aspect of literature. Halliday, in his literature on functional grammar, elaborates on three important functions of language: the ideational, the interpersonal, and the textual. The discourse of literature, especially of fiction, is characterized by four types of interaction. One, the text and the reader interact with each other. Two, characters interact with one another. Three, characters interact with the reader. Four, the author interacts with the reader. Obviously, all these interactions take place through language. The author and his characters perceive the world around them in their own personal, subjective, idiosyncratic ways. We call this the phenomenological view of language. The author-reader, character-character and character-reader communication is dominated by interpersonal relationship. Finally, unless these various types of interaction are in some way organized properly, communication becomes problematic.

Every text, and literary text is no exception to this, has seven features: intentionality, acceptability, situationality, informativity, intertexuality, cohesion and coherence. Let us spend some time explaining these characteristics of a literary work.

The author of a literary work has an *intention*. S/he may aim at one or more of the following purposes: entertainment, instruction, persuasion, warning, etc. In the case of moralistic or didactic literature, the aim is quite explicit. In other types of literature, the reader has to read between and beyond the lines and discover the author's hidden agenda. Intentionality refers to the author.

The second feature of a work of literature is its *acceptability*. A text has to be acceptable to the readers as far as its theme, language and style are concerned. When a text is unacceptable to a section of readership, it is banned. D.H. Lawrence's *Lady Chatterley's Lover*, Nathaniel Hawthorne's *Scarlet Letter*, Salman Rushdie's *Midnight's Children* and Taslima Nasreen's *Lajja* were not acceptable to various sections of the society for different reasons.

Thirdly, a text has a *situation* wherein characters act and converse. It is the situation, which acts as the centripetal force and connects various actions and interactions. For example, Mulk Raj Anand's *Untouchable* revolves around the pathetic situation in which the protagonist of the novel, Bakha, is lodged.

Fourthly, a text unfolds through continuous filtration of given information and addition of new *information*. This is what informativity means. The information provided may be true or false. In fact, the truth-value of the information presented in literature is that of another kind. That is why Aristotle in his *Poetics* says that literature is more universal than history. I.A. Richards in his critical writings makes a distinction between statements made in science and pseudo-statements made in literature. He adds that scientific statements can be verified in a laboratory, but literary statements cannot be; however, this does not mean that literary statements are false. For example, when a poet says, "My love is like a red, red rose," he does not mean that his lover is as red and as fragrant as a rose; what he means is that she is beautiful and fresh. It would be absurd to look for exactly the same qualities in the girl as a rose has.

Fifthly, the different parts of a literary work are interconnected. The beginning leads to the middle and the middle results into the ending. The outcome is an organic whole. T.S. Eliot in one of his poems says that the present was present in the past and the future is in the womb of the present, and the present and the future were present in the past. Let me use an analogy from genetic science. For example, where was a person before s/he was born. The answer is that s/he was genetically present in his/her parents. And where were his/her children before they were born? Obviously, they were genetically present in the grandparents. We can say more or less the same thing about the beginning, the middle, and the ending of a literary work. In other words, the beginning of a literary work determines its middle and its middle determines its ending. This is one meaning of *intertextuality*. Intertextuality requires that the various parts of a literary work (micro-texts) stay in harmony with one another by means of explicit grammatical and lexical connections. However, these links are not always explicit. Sometimes they occur in the form of meaning nexus or network. The explicit nexus in the form of grammar and vocabulary is called *cohesion* whereas semantic connectedness is described as *coherence*. There is another and more prevalent meaning of intertextuality, which is close to T.S.

Eliot's notion of interconnectedness between tradition and individual works of literature.

So, when we read a story, a poem, a one-act play or a full-length play, we can evaluate it with reference to the seven characteristics. But, that is just one approach. Another way to look at literature would be to look for freshness of expression. Literature uses hyper-semanticized language. This is particularly true of poetry. For example, there is no unusualness in expressions such as 'an hour ago,' 'a month ago,' etc. They have been used so often that they have lost their markedness. They have become routinized. On the contrary, when we encounter a phrase like 'a grief ago,' we linger over it for some time and our attention rivets on it because of its uncommonness. This sort of collocation is called 'deviation.' Sometimes we come across grammatical deviation like in the following lines from the well-known American poet, E.E. Cummings:

> yes is a pleasant country
> if's wintry
> (my lovely)
> let's open the year

These lines form a part of a lover's appeal to his sweetheart. On a close reading of the lines we notice that the poet has taken liberties with the syntax of the English language. In ordinary language, the subject position in the first two lines is occupied by the name of a country (France is a pleasant country, Iceland is a wintry country.). The question that arises is: Does the poet lack proficiency in English? Obviously, he does not. Then, why does he flout the rules of English grammar? Evidently, he does that because he has a special message to convey. Had he not violated the norms of English usage, he would have been left with no choice but to paraphrase the message: "When you use affirmative language, I feel warm; but when you speak in conditional language, with lots of buts and ifs, I feel cold." Consequently, his message would have lost its impact.

Discourse Approach

In the preceding section we discussed how literature could be studied using the framework of text-linguistics. Now let us talk about how literary discourse can be studied in the light of speech act theory, politeness principle, and cooperative principle (see Patil 1989a, 1989b, 1991, 1993, 1994, 1995, 1996, 1999, 2005, 2008).

Austin (1962, 1971, 1973), and Searle (1969, 1971, 1975, 1980) talk about speech acts. They discuss direct and indirect speech acts. Let me cite an everyday example. Let us imagine Rahul and Jayant engaged in a conversation about a box of sweets. Rahul asks Jayant where his box of sweets is. Jayant may choose to answer the query in a direct manner and say, "Sachin ate your sweets." Alternatively, he may prefer to be non-committal and say one of the following things:

> Sachin was feeling hungry.
> I saw Sachin opening the fridge.
> Where is the snow of last year?
> Show me your diet sheet, please!

Thus utterances can be arranged on a continuum of directness and indirectness. However, each speech act can be considered from three angles: locution, illocution, and perlocution. Locution refers to the actual production of an utterance. For example, when we say something in English, we combine English sounds to form words and English words to make sentences, which we utter using our vocal organs. However, we speak in order to inform, persuade, frighten, warn and advise. This intention is the illocutionary act, which refers to the intention of the speaker. When the speaker succeeds in informing, persuading, advising, scaring, etc., his illocutionary act achieves its perlocutionary impact on the addressee. We can assess conversations in a novel or a play in the light of speech act theory. Elam (1980) outlines a very systematic approach to the study of theatre and drama, and demonstrates how application of speech act theory can produce insightful analyses of theatrical performances and dramatic discourses.

Grice (1975) provides another perspective on the study of literature. He discusses the following maxims of conversation: (a) Maxim of Quantity: Let's not make our contribution more informative or less informative than it is necessary. In other words, let's not offer more information; let's not offer less information. (b) Maxim of Quality: Let's tell the truth. Let's not tell lies. Let's not say something for which we don't have evidence. (c) Maxim of Relation: Let's offer relevant contribution. Let's not digress. (d) Maxim of Manner: Let's speak clearly. Let's not speak ambiguously.

We can analyze conversations in a novel or a play with reference to the observance or violation of cooperative principle. Characters in literature as well as in real life float the four maxims of conversational cooperation for a purpose. For example, they want to avoid face-threatening acts, or they want to be non-committal, sarcastic, humorous, etc. Life will be drab and literature will have no aesthetic value if all of us observe the cooperative principle all the time.

Another perspective comes from Lakoff (1973), who outlines the politeness principle in the following manner: In our everyday life, we interact with family, friends, acquaintances, colleagues, strangers etc. We need to be careful while conversing with them. Each one of us has a "face" or image or status. When we pay compliments, express gratitude to others, extend invitation to them, apologize to them, we protect their faces, appease them, and make them feel good. Such strategies are positive politeness strategies. When we criticize them, complain against them, encroach on their privacy and freedom, use aggravating language with them, we threaten their face. Such behaviour is called negative politeness behaviour. There is nothing like absolute politeness. The two important principles governing our interaction are 'solidarity principle' and 'power principle.' It is difficult to talk about polite behaviour in absolute terms. The politeness or impoliteness of behaviour depends on who says what to whom, when and where. What is polite in the context of one type of relationship may not be so in the context of another. By the same token, what is polite in one culture may not be so in another culture. Any everyday discourse and literary discourse can be studied in the light of politeness principle.

Linguistic-Functional Nativization Approach

The non-native creative authors had to reinvent the English language to authentically present their culture. Now, the legitimate question here is "what is a reinvented language?" A language that is transplanted from its native soil to an alien soil is a reinvented language. We can say that such a language is born again in the sense that it has to carry the weight of new cultural experiences. English is a twice-born language in the socio-cultural context of India. It is a once-born language in those countries where it is used as a native language. One can think of the use of the English in terms of three circles: the inner circle, the outer circle and the expanding circle. English is a once-born language in the countries that belong to the inner circle whereas it is a twice-born language in the contexts of the countries in the outer and expanding circles. Non-native varieties of the English language are characterized with sociolinguistic or pragmatic transfer. The use of rules of speaking and writing from one's own native speech community when speaking and writing in a second or foreign language is known as sociolinguistic or pragmatic transfer. There are two types of transfer: unconscious or unintentional and conscious or intentional. (Pandharipande 1987: 155) Learners of English as a second/foreign language, for instance, unconsciously transfer the rules of use from their mother tongue. Similarly, general users of English in India unwittingly impose the rules of their mother tongue on the other tongue. Characters in Indian English novels, for example, are producers of unconscious deviation. On the other hand, creative writers are conscious creators of deviation from standard variety of English. The very idea of a standard implies stability. But language is of its nature unstable. It is essentially protean in nature, adapting its shape to suit changing circumstances. It would otherwise lose its vitality and its communicative and communal value. The users of English fashion it to their need, thereby demonstrating a high degree of linguistic capability. The innovation indicates that

English has been learned, not just as a set of fixed conventions to conform to, but also as an adaptable resource for making meaning. And making meaning is a personal as well as communal activity. The creative users of English as a second or foreign language are proficient in that language to the extent that they possess it, make it their own, bend it to their will, assert themselves through it, rather than submit to the dictates of its form. They take possession of the language, turn it to their advantages, and make it real for them. This is what mastery means. So, in a way, proficiency only comes with non-conformity, when people can take the initiative and strike out on their own. Let us consider these remarks of the Nigerian writer, Achebe: "I feel that the English language will be able to carry the weight of my African experience. . . . But it will have to be a new English, still in communion with its ancestral home but altered to suit its new African surroundings" (62).

Achebe is a novelist, and he is talking here about creative writing. But what he says clearly has wider relevance and applies to varieties of English elsewhere. The point is that all uses of language are creative in the sense that they draw on linguistic resources to express different perceptions of reality. English is called upon to carry the weight of all kinds of experience, much of it very remote indeed from its ancestral home. The new English, which Achebe refers to, is locally developed.

And this point applies to all other new varieties of English, which have been created to carry the weight of different experiences in different surroundings. All non-native writers of English literature write with an accent,' as it were. From the level of lexical redefinition to that of stylistic features and discourse arrangement and speech functions, the text is marked as non-native. (Nelson 1985: 245)

In the present section of the paper we would like to focus attention on speech functions. As we know, speech functions are specific to speech communities. Different cultures have different ways of doing things with words. Asians, for example, have their own ways of saying and meaning things in English. Ma (1966: 257) cites an interesting observation: A General Motors manager once expressed his frustration to a friend of the author by saying, "I don't understand you Asians. You say 'no' when you are supposed to say 'yes' and say 'yes' when you are supposed to say 'no.'" To put it differently, Asians have nativized English. The term 'nativization' has been described variously as acculturation, indigenization or hybridization of a language in a non-native socio-cultural context. The term is used to describe the divergence of varieties of a language from a parent source. In the context of English, the term 'nativization' refers to the changes, which English has undergone as a result of its contact with various languages in diverse cultural and geographical settings.

Now let us see a few examples of this markedness, with specific reference to two speech functions in Indian English novels: complimenting and blessing. For the sake of focus, the illustrations are selected from Rama Mehta's *Inside the Haveli*, a representative Indian English novel. Literary sources can provide valuable data for identifying culture-specific speech act effects. These data are perfectly authentic in that they were not specifically produced for speech act analysis. They are produced in writing because, in the judgement of the author, they simulate actual conversations in real-life situations (Kachru 1992: 239). Now, let us illustrate this with the speech function of complimenting.

A compliment contains a positive evaluation and conveys the complimenter's desire to make the complimentee feel good; it indebts the complimentee, obliging her to repay the debt in some way. As Pomerantz (1978) remarks, the act of responding to compliments is constrained by these two conditions: (i) agree with the complimenter, (ii) avoid self-praise. Since a compliment always contains a positive evaluation, the two conditions conflict with each other. For, it is difficult to agree with the complimenter and avoid self-praise at the same time. When one accepts a compliment, one indirectly praises oneself, thus violating the second condition. When one rejects a compliment, one expresses disagreement with the complimenter, thus flouting the first condition.

This dilemma has to be overcome if a compliment is to achieve its social objective or perform its functions. The most important function of compliments is to increase or consolidate the solidarity between the interlocutors. Compliments act as social lubricants: they serve to establish and maintain camaraderie. Since complimenting addresses the positive face needs of the compliment giver, the compliment receiver is forced, as it were, to accept such a favour and to express his gratitude for it, since rejecting runs counter to saving the positive face of the compliment giver. The rejection of a compliment challenges the evaluative judgement of the compliment giver, but it also reassures the compliment giver that the compliment receiver is not willing to be set on a level above the compliment giver. Apparently, there seems to be no way to avoid self-praise entitled by accepting compliments without engaging in the other—disagreement entailed by rejecting them. Returning a compliment offers the responder a way out by partially meeting the two conditions at once. This can be seen as a direct result of the indebting nature of compliments. It helps the responder to get out of the debt by returning the verbal gift to the compliment giver.

Different cultures employ different compliment response strategies. Responses to compliments also reflect the value system of the particular speech community. The 'Why' of compliments and compliment responses is usually assumed to be culturally universal: compliments are offered with a view to making the hearer/receiver of compliments feel happy. The how of compliments, on the other hand, seems to be culture-bound. Some cultures might sound in their use of compliments as obsequious, diffident and miserly; others might sound unappreciative and smug, generous and prolific. We can prepare cultural value profiles of societies on the basis of compliments. Let us look at the following compliment and response to it from *Inside the Haveli* as culturally loaded speech acts:

> 'Where is Binniji?' asked the wife of Daulat Singhji. 'Hukkum, you have been blessed with many things but *your daughter-in-law is the haveli's greatest ornament.*'

> 'You have always been generous in your praises for this haveli,' replied Bhagwat Singhji's wife with customary humility.

The compliment giver describes the object of compliment, the daughter-in-law, as the 'greatest ornament of the haveli.' This compliment, like any other compliment, serves as an expression of approval. Its social function is reaffirmation or establishment of common ground, mutuality or solidarity. But the most striking feature of the compliment content is the comparison of the daughter-in-law with an ornament. In some other culture, it might be taken as an insult and as an attempt to reduce the object of compliment to the level of an inanimate object. But in the context of Indian socio-cultural values and beliefs, it is an absolutely positive speech act. In order to understand the positive implications of the compliment, one has to go beyond the semantic or propositional content of the compliment and discover the pragmatic content. We distinguish different levels of analysis of compliments, greetings, blessings, and so on: (i) semantic content level or propositional content level, (ii) pragmatic function or illocutionary force potential and, (iii) sociolinguistic level (Davies 1987: 78). It is obvious that the compliment is a twice-born one. Its semantic force and pragmatic implications are in fact sociolinguistic transfers from Indian languages to English.

Now let me say a word about the compliment response. If the recipient of the compliment had accepted it in a straightforward way, she would have been dubbed impolite or arrogant. Similarly, if she had rejected it, she would have been considered unappreciative. Therefore, she finds a way out. She accepts that her daughter-in-law is the greatest ornament of the haveli, but then says that it is the compliment giver's generosity that makes her think so highly of the daughter-in-law. The principle that operates in compliments and compliment responses in Indian English is this: the speakers elevate the status of the hearers and humble themselves. One of the popular politeness strategies in many countries and cultures is addressor lowering and addressee elevation through verbal means. And this strategy seems similar to bowing one's head or knees in prayer or supplication. The deliberate status-distancing that one speaker tries to emphasize between the interacting duo is intended to develop a positive attitude toward the speaker and serve as a subtle means of pressure to attain a particular goal. (Mehrotra 1996: 107). Now, let us illustrate nativization at the level of the speech function of blessing.

A blessing is an expression wishing the hearer well. It may be a prayer divine intervention, favour or bestowal of spiritual, material or social prosperity. It may also be a prayer for longevity or reproductive fertility. Blessings acquire their signification within the context of social and cultural norms and institutions. All literature carries with it implicit assumptions about what is acceptable, important, holy and repugnant. Lazar (1993: 65-66) offers a list of thirteen aspects of culture, which can be a useful starting-point in reading literary texts from any culture. They are as follows:

(i) objects or products that exist in one society, but not in another, e.g., cucumber sandwiches;
(ii) social structures, roles and formulaic expressions which embody cultural values, e.g. "Marriages are made in heaven"
(iii) social structures, roles and relationships, e.g., superwomen;
(iv) customs/ rituals/ traditions/ festivals, e.g., arranged marriages;
(v) beliefs/values/superstitions;
(vi) political, historic and economic background;
(vii) institutions;
(viii) taboos;
(ix) metaphorical/connotative meaning, e.g., "doing harijan work";
(x) humour;
(xi) representativeness;
(xii) genre; and
(xiii) the status of the written language.

And literaure is written in language. Hence it is axiomatic to say that language reflects aspects of culture. Of course, not every word reflects culture. For example, one can say that genders do not reflect culture--Russian has three genders, French has two, and English has none. But there are certain lexical items (e.g. honorifics) and parts of language, which have to do with the relationship between the speaker and the addressee that are revealing of the respective culture. (Wierzbicka 1986: 351)

Of the thirteen aspects listed above, the most relevant to the purpose of the present paper is "formulaic expressions which embody cultural values." Blessings, like compliments, are formulaic expressions, highly conventionalized forms of language, and they have to do with the relationship between the speaker and the addressee. People exchange blessings in greetings, thanks and leave-takings. Blessings, like compliments, function as expressions of solidarity, approval, and good will. This is the universal aspect of blessings. The content, however, varies from culture to culture. Though certain things like happiness and longevity might be universal topics, there are certain culture-bound topics. Let us look at the following examples from *Inside the Haveli*:

(i) *God bless you.* We are proud of your success. May you continue to excel in your studies. (174)

(ii) Vijay Bai Sa, *God bless her*, is the daughter of this haveli. (79)

(iii) May you *have eight sons*. (16)

(iv) May you *have many sons* and may you always wear red. (29)

(v) May you *have eight sons*; may the gods bless you. May this haveli flourish forever. (29)

(vi) May you always *wear red* and live to *see your great grandsons*. (72)

(vii) May you always *wear red* and may *your sons carry on the illustrious name of this haveli*. (161)

(viii) Binniji . . . God bless you. May you always *wear red.* May gold always shine on your hands. (208)

(ix) May you *live in your husband's shadow* for a hundred years. (86)

The first two blessings are neutral. In other words, they may be exchanged in any culture. The rest of the blessings, however, are different. There are two frequent topics of blessings: (a) wish for the addressee's and/or her husband's longevity, and (b) prayer for the addressee's fertility. A lady who passes away before her husband is considered lucky. She 'wear red' till the end of her life. It is interesting that a woman carries with her the mark of being married whereas a man does not carry with him such a mark. She walks and 'lives in her husband's shadow.' Secondly, a woman would long to be a mother. Hence the blessing "may you have eight/many sons." A woman without children, especially without sons, is looked upon rather differently. It is interesting that all fertility blessings mention 'sons' and not 'daughters.' A son is traditionally regarded as a carrier of the name of the family. This reflects the attitude of the respective speech community towards women and it has implications of a woman's secondary role and status in that society. In our society, the place of woman in reality has always been secondary although woman has been eulogized in literatures of different types. Also, it is worth nothing that the recipients of some of these blessings are only women. Men never receive the following blessings:

(i) 'May you always live in the shadow of your wife.'
(ii) 'May you always wear red/white.'
(iii) 'May you have eight sons.'

The fact that these blessings are addressed only to women indicates the role of women in our society: to perpetuate lineage and to be always obedient to the husband as one's shadow is to one. Thus, these blessings reflect our cultural assumptions, belief and value systems and our views on the position, status, and role of men and women in our society. These things are available to a reader who takes pains to examine the history and biography of formulaic expressions such as blessings, and discover the hidden cultural and sociological agenda underlying them.

To sum up, stylistics is of great help to teachers and students of literature. It increases our understanding and enjoyment of literature. It also sensitizes us to the subtleties, nuances and beautiful aspects of the linguistic side of literature. Incidentally, a word of caution is in order here. Excessive application of stylistics can kill the aesthetically satisfying spirit of literature. A judicious use of stylistics can help students to understand and appreciate literature and can enhance their literary, linguistic, and communicative competence.

Bibliography

Achebe, C. "The African writer and the English language," *Morning yet on Creation Day*. London: Heinemann, 1975.

Austin, J.L. *How to Do Things with Words*. New York: Oxford University Press, 1962.

___. (1971) "Performative-Constative." In, J.R. Searle, ed. *The Philosophy of Language*. Oxford: Oxford University Press, 13-22.

___. (1973) "Speech Acts" In, J.B.P. Allen and S.P. Corder, eds. *Readings for Applied Linguistics*. Oxford: Oxford University Press, 1973, 37-52.

Davies, E.E. (1987) "A Contrastive Approach to the Analysis of Politeness Formulas," *Applied Linguistics*, 8 (1), 75-88

Elam, K. (1980) *The Semiotics of Theatre and Drama*. London and New York: Methuen

Grice, H.P. (1975) "Logic and Conversation." In P. Cole and T.L. Morgan, eds. *Syntax and Semantics*. New York: Academic Press, 44-45.

Kachru, Y. (1992) "Speech acts in the other tongue: an integrated approach to cross-cultural research." *World Englishes*, 11 (2/3), 235-40

Lakoff, R.T. (1973) "The Logic of Politeness: Minding Your P's and Q's." *The Papers from the Ninth Regional Meeting of the Chicago Linguistic Society*, 292-305.

Lazar, G. (1993) *Literature and Language Teaching*. Cambridge: Cambridge University Press.

Ma, R. (1996) "Saying 'yes' for 'no' and 'no' for 'yes': A Chinese rule." *Journal of Pragmatics*. 25, 257-66.

Mehrotra, R.R. (1996) "How to be polite in Indian English." *International Journal for Sociology of Language*, 11, 99 110.

Nelson, C.L (1985) "My language, your culture: Whose communicative competence?" *World Englishes*, 4 (2), 243-50.

Ojaide, T. (1987) My poetry: English language and the African tradition." *World Englishes*, 6 (2), 165-67.

Pandharipande, R. (1987) "On nativazation of English." In *World Englishes*, 6 (2), 149-58.

___. (1992) "Defining politeness in Indian English." *World Englishes*, 11 (2/3), 241-50.

Patil, Z.N. (1989a). The Use of Aggravating Language in Indian Novels in English. *Indian Journal of English Studies*, 28, 13-20.

___. (1989b). Novels of Mulk Raj Anand: A Sociolinguistic Study: U.S. Bahri, ed. *Papers in Language and Linguistics, 2*. 78-92). New Delhi: Bahri Publishers.

___. (1991). "Style in Rama Mehta's *Inside the Haveli*" R.K. Dhawan, ed. *Indian Women Novelists, I (V)* 16-30. New Delhi: Prestige.

___. (1993). "A Sociolinguistic Analysis of Jai Nimbkar's *Temporary Answers.*" R.K. Dhawan, ed. *Indian Women Novelists, I (1)* 236-49. New Delhi: Prestige.

___. (1994). *Style in Indian English Fiction: A study in politeness strategies*. New Delhi: Prestige.

___. (1995). "Sarala Barnabas' *The Promise of Spring*: A socio-pragmatic Analysis." R.K. Dhawan ed. *Indian Women Novelists III (4)* 210-22. New Delhi: Prestige.

___. (1996). "Expressions of Politeness in Indian English Novels." *Indian Linguistics*, 57 (1-4), 141-52

___. (1999). "A Once Born Literature in a Twice Born Language." K.V. Tirumalesh, ed. *Language Matters: Essays on language, literature, and translation,* 41-58. New Delhi: Allied.

___. (2005). "Twice Born Languages: A perspective on English in Asia." A paper presented at Kyoto Conference on Asian Englishes, Kyoto University of Foreign Languages, Kyoto, Japan.

___. (2008) *Indian English Novel: A stylistic approach*. New Delhi: Prestige.

Pomerantz, A. (1978) "Compliment responses: Notes on the cooperation of multiple constraints." J. Schenkein, ed. *Studies in Organization of Conversational Interaction*. New York: Academic Press, 79-112.

Searle, J.R. (1969) *Speech Acts: An essay in the philosophy of language*. Cambridge: Cambridge University Press.

___. (1971) "Austin on Locutionary and Illocutionary Acts." J. Rosenberg, & C. Travis, eds. *Readings in Philosophy of Language*. Englewood Cliffs: Prentice-Hall.

___. (1975) "Indirect Speech Acts." P. Cole, & J.L. Morgan, eds. *Syntax and Semantics, Vol. 3, Speech Acts*, 59-85.

___. (1880) "What is a Speech Act?" A.K. Pugh, V.J. Lee and J. Swann, eds. *Language and Language Use*, 312-27.

Wierzbicka, A. (1986) "Does language reflect culture? Evidence from Australian English." *Language in Society*, 15 (3), 349-74.

Traditional Style Analysis of Kamala Markandaya's Fiction

VIPASHA AGARWAL

Kamla Markandaya is one of the well known Indian novelists writing in English. She won international fame and recognition with the publication of her maiden novel, *Nectar in a Sieve* (1954). Margaret P. Joseph has rightly pointed out that the thematic pattern in Kamala Markandaya's novel explores the suffering out of "the struggle between the traditional and the modern, the individual and the society, or one race and another" (1).

It is said that the style of an author is the image of his mind. Markandaya's mental image is the image of her characters. The novel *Nectar in a Sieve* starts in a flashback mode with Rukmani, the woman narrator reflecting on the sequence of events in the evening her life. She is the single uniting force in the whole novel. As she removes the curtains of time, she remembers her husband Nathan whom she loved dearly. "Sometimes at night I think that my husband is with me again, coming gently through the mists and we are tranquil together" (2). The words set the tone of a reverie.

As she moves back, she translates the emptiness of her heart after Ira's marriage and the departure of guests in short, simple sentences: "Then it was all over, the bustle, the laughter, the noise. The wedding guests departed. The throng melted" (38). The language is poetic when she is happy and content and her heart sang. "While the sun shines on you and the fields are green and beautiful to the eye and your husband sees beauty in you which no one has seen before, and you have a good store of grain laid away . . . my heart sang and my feet were light as I went about my work." (7) The rhythmic flow of words, the long sentences joined by conjunction, correspond to Rukmani's feelings of happiness and satisfaction.

In her language, we find an occasional, random use of Indian words like *dhal, kum kum, dhoti, maidan, ghee, jutka, namaste, pakora, nimbu paani, colam, bania* and the like. These words are italicized and are explained separately. They give a distinct Indian touch to her writings but Markandaya writes for her Western readers as much as for Indians. "Markandaya's divided loyalty to the place of her birth and her stay is reflected in her non-committal language which has the fusion of an ounce of East and many pounds of West, of an occasional sprinkling of an Indian in a huge heap of English words" (3).

It is also interesting to note that as an excellent fictional artist, Markandaya has depicted the existential dilemma, despair and anguish of her characters by using artistic devices of imagery and symbolism. Rukmani, the youngest daughter of the village landlord, dreams of a great wedding, but her hopes are shattered when she has to marry Nathan—a landless farmer. Around Nathan's hut hangs a garland of mango leaves which is a symbol of prosperity. The garland, however, is dry, symbolizing their withered future. The image proves to be a peep into the future of this farmer couple's life and their labour destroyed by the vagaries of weather or the calamities of life. They cannot enjoy the nectar of their labour as it passes through the sieve. As we read the novel, we read how year after year Nathan's labour is wasted; their land is claimed by tannery, their sons leave them, they come to the city in search of Murugan, who is never found and Rukmani goes back to the village without Nathan.

The kitchen garden so well nurtured by Rukmani, full of vegetables, symbolizes hope and happiness but the snake in it is a symbol of evil. Nathan kills it and that proves to be his albatross. The snake destroys their proverbial Garden of Eden. The advent of tannery stands for industrialization. The destructive role played by tannery is indicated very convincingly. Rukmani does not like the 'clatter and clamour,' 'the stench of skins,' because they replace 'the clear soft greens that had once coloured our village . . . cleaving its cool silences with clamour' (134). "The tannery represents a world of immortality, greed and corruption invading another which is moral, happy and pure" (4).

The novel being a tale of rural life is full of images from rural life and nature. Nathan advises Rukmani to 'bend like the grass' (28), Kuti's thin body is compared to 'a handful of leaves in an untended garden' (118), tannery spreads like weeds. Rukmani, during her pregnancy is compared to a 'water buffalo' (14). Ira when happy is 'like a bird' (119) and so on. Kamala Markandaya is always conscious of using the right words according to the situation and character. However, she has not Indianized English. Her novels have a few Indian words scattered here and there. In a world where it is fashionable to have an Indian flavour in English, Markandaya continues to be an orthodox perfectionist who maintains the inviolable purity of language.

Light and dark imagery is also used with light signifying hope, happiness, rich harvest and dark, misery, death and disease. Deepawali with its lamps, fireworks and flames on a dark night brings a feeling of happiness and jubilation to one and all. When Rukmani returns happy in the night, with the assurance given by Kenny that Ira's barrenness can be cured, very aptly, "full moon was shining." Ira's child Sacrabani, is an illegitimate child and hence cannot face sunlight. Markandaya, however, gives a scientific explanation to this by telling her readers that he is an albino child. When Nathan and Rukmani are forced to leave the village and go to the city in search of their son, Murugan, they are helped by the yellow light of a lantern which is symbolically unable to dispel the darkness. We read that their journey to the city proves futile. The 'yellow flare' of the temple attracts them promising 'food and shelter' (146). They get it but at the cost of their possessions. The yellow glare on the temple, according to M.K. Bhatnagar, stands for deceit (5). They enter the temple, 'helped by the yellow flare,' but after Nathan's death, the yellow flare is quenched, bringing an end to the deceits in her life. Hospital and Dr. Kenny stand for basic goodness, which can be seen in society. It is interesting to note that the hospital, a charitable institution and meant for the good of the people, grows at a very slow pace while the tannery—an evil one—grows at an astonishing speed signifying the ever-growing evils like greed and corruption.

There are house images in the novel. The doctor's house with 'its doors and windows wide open' (155) signifies the warm welcome they receive but the title is justified because they are not able to find their son. The collector's house 'on a hill top' images their high hopes of finding Murugan but again their efforts prove futile. The house image in *A Handful of Rice* is also symbolic. Ravi, a young man, who comes from his village, to the city in search of a living and for better prospects, is seen lost in the city. Acute hunger drives him to desperation and he breaks open the rusty bars of Apu's window, enters the room and demands not only food but also a bed. Apu and his wife Jayamma, initially yield to Apu's threats, but later when he is resting, tie him down with a bicycle chain and cotton sari. Ravi unsuccessfully tries to free himself from the cycle chain, symbolizing his fight against the society at a later stage. Just like the metallic chain, the society gags the weak. It has no emotions or feelings. The cotton sari, with which his arms are bound, is also a soft, yet powerful chain. This stands for his subsequent marriage to Nalini- Apu's daughter and her strong influence on Ravi. She remains his most powerful force in adverse circumstances. She holds the key to Ravi's happiness. Jayamma and Nalini, the two women of two different generations, stand for society and family respectively. Jayamma is harsh and callous like the society while Nalini is kind and affectionate and brings a lot of positive change in him.

Apu and Jayamma, at another level, stand for the older generation while Nalini and Ravi for the new one. Apu is a worldly wise man who believes in hard work, taking the ups and downs of life stoically and is himself honest, though he has to indulge in flattery and bribery. Ravi is energetic, has dreams, aspirations but lacks tolerance and humility symbolizing the traits of youth. Apu's death means the passing away of the older generation. Ravi becomes the head of the family. Ravi, in his urge to earn quick money, fails miserably because the competitive world of business symbolized by Damodar is full of violence.

Markandaya uses jungle imagery for the city again and again. Here might is right and a place where man's identity gets completely lost. Ravi is unfit for this jungle because he has to save the honour of his family, and fight the pangs of his own conscience. A.V. Krishna Rao says, "Damodar symbolizes a certain kind of freedom—a freedom that is completely self-centred and divorced from ethical sensibility. He is a law unto himself. Since money holds the key to the chambers of possessive pleasure, Damodar should get rich quick by whatever means available. In contrast, Nalini symbolizes the subtle fragrance of life, a clean, healthy and traditional life. She promises 'sweet life' but demands hard and honest labour (6). Ravi becomes a citizen of this unreal city signifying a lifestyle that is abstract, empty, corrupt and highly competitive. Rice stands for survival. His struggle to reach for a handful of rice denotes his struggle for survival in this city which is neither dying nor living.

The Nowhere Man depicts the crisis of alienation and the loss of identity of Srinivas who is presented as 'a figure of loneliness,' 'an intruder' who, even after staying for fifty years in England, feels like a 'nowhere man.' The novel is rich in house imagery. The house which is 'an image of brick and mortar' (7) symbolizes his imprisonment. It stands for the end of his freedom. He cannot go anywhere and symbolically dies in front of his house. The 'grimy curtains' and 'peeling paint' of the house after Vasantha's death image the threads and glamour of life falling apart. Srinivas's efforts to bridge the Oriental-Occidental gap and become one with the natives are symbolized in the house. Vasantha, his wife, believed in "Vasudhaiv Kutumbakam" and the house stands for that when Srinivas rents it out to the white and the brown. Though it crashes Vasantha's dream of giving the first floor to Laxman and his family, the second to Seshu and his family, but Srinivas's act of assembling people of different racial groups in one house raises him to a different level. The leprosy from which Srinivas suffers, strongly symbolizes identity crisis and the subsequent feeling of alienation.

Madhusudan Prasad characterizes it as "symbolic of the spiritual leprosy that corrodes the value of England" (8).

A.V. Krishna Rao says, "If Srinivas suffers from the leprosy of body, Fred and his gang suffer from the leprosy of the soul" (9). Srinivas's ostracization is complete when his house is set on fire by Fred, the evil son of his good neighbour. In his death, Srinivas, for V. Rangam, becomes a symbol of "millions of men who for some reason or the other leave their own roots and fail to strike roots in the alien soil, and die as rootless and restless individuals. Srinivas lives in England for one full generation only to be a nowhere man" (10). The collapse of the house and its owner signals the end of Srinivas's quest for identity. When Fred gets trapped in his own fire, the blackman, Srinivas's tenant, notices him but decides not to rescue him. He is burnt to death. This symbolizes the forecast of the novelist that the suppressed will get victory over the oppressors one day, regaining their identity.

Thus, in the works of Kamala Markandaya, rootlessness, divergent cultural backgrounds, poverty, hunger and advent of modernity play an important role in the lives of people. However, in spite of the melancholy produced, her characters do not get swept off their feet and somehow they maintain a balance. All is not lost, there is still a ray of hope; this is what the novelist seems to say.

Works Cited

A.V. Krishna Rao. "Continuity and change in the novels of Kamala Markandaya," *Perspectives on Kamala Markandaya*. Ed. Madhusudan Prasad. Ghaziabad: Vimal, 1984.

_____. *The Nowhere Man*. Bombay: Orient Longman, 1973.

_____. *Nectar in a Sieve*. Mumbai: Jaico, 2001.

M.K. Bhatnagar. *Kamala Markandaya—A Critical Spectrum*. New Delhi: Atlantic, 2002.

Madhusudan Prasad, "Introduction," *Perspectives on Kamala Markandaya*. Ghaziabad: Vimal, 1984.

Margaret P. Joseph. *Kamala Markandaya*. New Delhi: Arnold Heinemann, 1980.

Ramesh K. Srivastava. *The Novels of Kamala Markandaya.* Amritsar: Guru Nanak Dev University, 1998.

_____. "Symbolism in *Nectar in a Sieve*," *Indian Scholar*, Volume 2, July 1979.

V. Rangam. "The Nowhere Man: A Critical Analysis" *Perspectives on Kamala Markandaya.* Ed. Madhusudan Prasad. Ghaziabad: Vimal, 1984.

A Comparative Study of Language Use in Anita Desai and Kiran Desai

JYOTI SINGH

Anita Desai is one of the leading novelists in the field of Indian English literature. She is known for unparalleled portrayals of psychological states of mind of her characters, who are mostly women. She won the 1978 Sahitya Akademi award for the novel *Fire on the Mountain*, which has been taken up for study in this paper. The literary world rued the fact that even though she was thrice nominated for the Booker prize, she could never really get it. This lack was more than fulfilled by her illustrious daughter Kiran Desai, who won the 2006 Man Booker prize, considered the highest literary award for fiction in the world, for her novel *The Inheritance of Loss*, which has also been taken up for study. A comparative study of the two much-acclaimed novels by the mother-daughter duo becomes a fascinating study. The study reveals many points of similarity and dissimilarity with regard to the thematic and stylistic aspects.

Both the writers—Anita Desai and her daughter Kiran Desai—have used stylistic devices in their novels very effectively. Anita Desai tries to convey her perception of life or, more precisely, the conditions of her characters and their psychological reactions to the situations they face through images and symbols. Her language is poetic, but the poetic touch found in *Cry, the Peacock* or the *Voices in the City* has somewhat yielded to, what Paul Scott calls "clear, cool prose." So far as the novel *The Inheritance of Loss* is concerned, not only are these thematic issues in the background responsible for the winning of Man Booker Prize, its prose is another attraction of the novel. She seems to be one up on her mother. Her sense of imagery is wonderful and her sentence construction has the poetic touch plus the broad sweep indicative of a cosmopolitan mind.

Anita Desai is known for the sensuous appeal of words, as Meenakshi Mukherjee has remarked: "Her language is marked by three characteristics: sensuous richness, a high-strung sensitiveness and a love for the sound of words" (Kundu 182). It is evocative, to say the least, and more direct than the language of the two novels referred to earlier in this passage. The critic Mohini Chakranarayan has conducted a stylistic study of Anita Desai's prose. She concludes: "Desai's sentence structure, use of proper and common nouns, of plosives and fricatives, careful use of words with pejorative meanings or passive connotations, different figures of speech, particularly metaphors, antitheses, zoological images, irony etc. contribute to and reinforce the thematic and structural patterns of the novel" (Kundu 184).

Since the major theme of her novels, including *Fire on the Mountain* is alienation, it is only natural that the images and symbols of alienation abound in her novel. In this novel, similes can be noticed in the expressions like "As straight as a rod" (*Fire on the Mountain*, hereafter abbreviated as FOM, 11). Further:

> Looking down, over all those years she had survived and borne, she saw them, not bare and shining as the plains below, but like the gorge cluttered, chocked and blackened with the heads of children and grandchildren, servants and guests, all restlessly surging, clamouring about her. (FOM 17)

> A burst of crackling and hissing, as of suddenly awakened geese, a brief silence, then a voice issued from it that made her gasp and shrivel, balling up her fingers tightly. (FOM 20)

Anita Desai has used bird imagery which brings out the gap between aspiration and experience. Nanda's desire for absolute freedom is defeated in the face of her domestic responsibilities:

> An eagle swept over it, far below her, a thousand feet below, its wings outspread, . . . she had wished to imitate that eagle- gliding with eyes closed. Then a cuckoo called, quite close, here in her garden, very softly, very musically, but definitely calling—she recognized its domestic tone. (FOM 19)

In *Fire on the Mountain*, the image of moon symbolizes the perverse nature of Raka. She is not enchanted by the beauty of moon; rather she prefers a forest fire. Moon is a metaphor for Raka, but there is nothing pretty or gentle about her. Nanda's mistaking forest fire for moon, even for a short while, is symbolically suggestive of her expectations of Raka. But later she understands that Raka is a volcano, waiting to burst on the world in full fury. "Just then, as if to illustrate her tale and prove it true, the moon did rise, a great copper-red moon" (FOM 100).

Both the writers have used stylistic devices in their novels very effectively. In the beginning of both the novels, there are similes based on the hilly areas and natural environment of the places. In Kiran Desai's *The Inheritance of Loss*, she has used the simile for Kanchenjunga peak: "Kanchenjunga smoking like a volcano or a cigar" (IOL 231) and "watched the invisible mountain sides opposite as the falling lanterns of drunks plummeted like shooting stars" (IOL 289) "Memories are like diamonds" (IOL 79). Kiran Desai has used the image of sunflower beautifully: "Mostly he sat on a folding chair, silently moving an expressionless face like sunflower, a blank handicapped insistence following the sun, the only goal left in his life to match the two" (IOL 143).

Kiran Desai has used variations in the use of metaphors in her novel: "A conference of old men with elegant goat faces, smoking bidis" (IOL 300). Besides, there are other figures of speech like objectification, as in the following lines: "The five peaks of Kanchenjunga turned golden with the kind of luminous light that made you feel, if briefly, that truth was apparent. All you needed to do was to reach out and pluck it." (IOL 324)

The moonlight becomes 'ghostly'; the net looks 'grey and spidery' the drive is *eerily silent* and the branches of the trees also turn to be *ghost-grey* to her distorted and distressed vision. Her plight is symbolized in the 'broken and discarded shuttle cock.' Nanda's sorrow and bitterness are projected in the agitated flight of a lapwing through the 'funeral' moonlight. The word 'funeral' hints at her dark, gloomy future. The image of moon, though signifying Nanda's gloom, is not as intense and functional. Symbolically she becomes like "that hunted, fearful bird, distracted and disturbing" (FOM 26). The word picture of the burnt house signifies Raka's own broken home. But it is more than that. It is symbolic of Raka's fractured self. It is that scorched self of Raka that waits for an explosion, a total annihilation of the rotten world, as it can no more bear the emptiness of life. Even Carignano, the most satisfying place she had ever lived in so far cannot pacify the pent-up fury in her: "It was as dry and clean as a nut but she burst from its shell like an impatient kernel, small and explosive." (FOM 91)

Both the writers have used phonological parallelisms (alliteration) in a very effective way. As in "Plodding Postman" (FOM 3), in the description of Nanda Kaul's physique, the writer has used alliteration very effectively: "She was grey, tall and thin and her silk sari made a sweeping, shivering sound and she fancied she could merge with the pine trees and be mistaken for one" (FOM 1).

Kiran Desai has also used alliteration to show the secular spirit of the cook who was no Buddhist but who paid obeisance to Dalai Lama: "The muffled thunder of prayer rumbled down the mountain as the mules and horses stepped, pom-pommed out of the fog, bells ringing, prayer flags flying from saddles" (IOL 84). In these lines, we find the subtle repetition of /au/ sound in 'mountain,' 'down' and /o/ sound in 'pom,' 'fog' and /f/ sound in 'flag,' 'flying' etc. Both the writers have used native wards to bring a realistic touch to their novels. In *Fire on the Mountain*, Hindi words are used by Ram lal like *biri* (FOM 78}, *Churail* (77), *langurs* (58), *Angrez sahibs* and *Mem Shahibs* (66) But Kiran Desai has, in *The Inheritance of Loss*, used Gujarati and accented English with plain Hindi words in order to give the impression of Indianness:

"Hai, Hai humara Kya hoga, hai, hai, humara kya hoga." (72)
"Bhai Dekho, aisa hai" (105)
"Angrez ki tarah. Angrez jaisa." (105)
"Kem Chho? Saaru Choo? Teme Samjho chho? (137).

Vocal traits or accentual word patterns can be noticed in the expression like "Mrs. Sen pronounced potato 'poEtato,' and tomato as Toematto'" (131). The representation of a drunkard's speech is quite realistic: "Gointa be a beeg man, reech man, what you say ya vanna nice cheekan karry" (147).

Language is foregrounded in both the novels. While Anita Desai is known for her poetic prose, Kiran Desai comes out as a worthy inheritor in this respect. Anita Desai's language, in her novel discussed here is poetic, but the poetic touch found in *Cry, the Peacock* or *Voices in the City* has somewhat yielded to, what Paul Scott calls "clear, cool prose." Still, the sensuous appeal of her words is beyond comparison. Her careful use of different figures of speech, particularly metaphors, antitheses, zoological images, irony etc. is seen here also. Images and symbols of alienation abound in her novel. Kiran Desai is not far behind in the use of images and symbols. Her language has a wider sweep. Once she sets out to write something, she wanders after every conceivable element connected to the subject has been roped in. Her use of alliteration, hybridization, onomatopoeia etc. is certainly fascinating.

Thus, the two novels have much in common, though the generation gap between the mother and the daughter does show itself in the choice of subjects and the use of language. Kiran Desai is indeed a worthy daughter of an illustrious mother.

Works Cited

Desai, Anita. *Fire on the Mountain*. Vintage, 1999.

Desai, Kiran. *The Inheritance of Loss*. New Delhi: Penguin, 2006.

Chakranarayan, Mohini. *Style Studies in Anita Desai*. New Delhi: Atlantic, 2000

Kundu, Rama. Anita Desai's *Fire on the Mountain*. New Delhi: Atlantic, 2005.

Tripathi, B.L. *Anita Desai: Dimensions of the Inner World*. New Delhi: Prestige, 2007.

A Close Study of Anita Desai's *Voices in the City*

MONICA BALYAN DAHIYA

Generally, a literary text is likely to be appreciated better if it is studied in parallel with stylistic analysis. It highlights the vital role of the linguistic features of the text. This contribution provides much to the development of literary criticism. A close study of novel is what stylistics tries to apply to the text of the novel. It is the quality and quantity of words used that determines the overall utility and aesthetic value of any piece of writing. Every factor is explored to convey the meaning: content, vocabulary, syntax, morphology, phonetics, etc. The present study attempts to explain that stylistics is a useful discipline which encourages logical and creative thought and can be transferred to many other areas of academic study. As Leech and Short put it: 'Stylistics tries to explore for pattern and system below the surface forms of language, to search for principles of meaning and language use, which activate and control the code.' (5)

Stylisticians believe that style is a matter of choice. Every writer has his own peculiar choice of words and structures which make his writing unique. Stylistics focuses on these particular choices of the writers in order to understand the underlying pattern. It has been rightly said: 'Stylistics is not a mechanical technique of style analysis. It acknowledges that intuition and personal judgment of the reader cannot be replaced by any method. The mystery of having been removed by words, as Dylan Thomas says, will always remain.' (5). One of the main tasks of stylistics is to check and validate intuition by methods of analysis. A detailed analysis of a prose piece will include careful study of the lexis, grammar, the schemes and tropes, cohesive and contextual devices, but the end is not mere objectivity. In this regard the point-to-point mathematical accuracy is not the aim. A rough indication of frequencies is generally a good guide to objective study. According to David Lodge, a novel critic can either isolate deliberately or at random, one or more passages and submit them to close exhaustive analysis, or trace significant threads through the language of an entire novel. "The first may be termed as the textural approach and the second structural. Textural criticism probably works most satisfactorily on the beginnings of the novels, as they are the only independent units in novels, since nothing else precedes them." Leech and Short also agree with this: 'A point of particular concentration is the beginning of the fiction, which, according to the principle above, ought to be the point of least pre-supposition.' (179)

A structural approach attempts to take into account the linguistic character of the whole work. Both the approaches have their own limitations. The great local variation of tone and verbal intensity makes it very difficult to subject a whole novel to exhaustive stylistic analysis. As it is observed: "The analysis of a great novel suffers from bitterness" (Leech and Short 3), i.e., at best the stylistic analysis of a novel can only be in bits and pieces. Considering the synthesis of two methods of analysis, a detailed method of textural analysis of 250 words of the beginning of two novels of Desai is taken. Studies based on structural appearance include narrative devices (plot, point of view, lyrical elements, and rhetorical elements etc.) A few style markers have been selected from the list prepared by the noted critics Geoffrey N. Leech and Michael H. Short in their work *Style in Fiction*, in order to carry out the textual analysis. It is essential to decide upon a definite path of study. These markers will guide the analysis. Briefly, the categories are as under:

A. Lexical Categories

(i) *General:* To see if the vocabulary is simple or complex, formal or colloquial, descriptive or evaluative, general or specific etc. The use of emotive or other associations of words, as opposed to their referential meaning, dialect or register, idioms etc.

(ii) *Nouns:* Are the nouns abstract or concrete? What kinds of abstract nouns occur, *e.g.*, nouns referring to events, perceptions, processes, moral qualities, social qualities? What use is made of proper names?

(iii) *Adjectives:* The frequency and nature of adjectives, as for example, restrictive or non-restrictive, attributive or predicative etc.

(iv) *Verbs:* The importance of verbs and their referents. Are they transitive, intransitive etc.?

(v) *Adverbs:* Are adverbs frequent? What semantic functions do they perform?

B. Grammatical Categories

(i) *Sentence types*: Declarative, questions, commands, exclamations, or minor sentence types (such as sentences with no verb)?

(ii) *Sentence Complexity*: The average sentence length, the ratio of dependent to independent clauses etc.

(iii) *Clause Types:* The types of dependent clauses are favoured—Relative clauses, adverbial clauses etc.

(iv) *Verb Phrases:* Are there any significant departures from the use of simple past tense?

(v) *Minor word Classes:* Prepositions, conjunctions, pronouns, determiners, auxiliaries, interjections etc.

(vi) *General:* Any general types of grammatical construction used for special effect?

C. Figures of Speech

(i) *Grammatical and lexical schemes:* Cases of formal and structural repetition (anaphora, parallelism etc.) and the rhetorical effect of these.

(ii) *Phonological schemes:* Are there any phonological patterns of rhyme, alliteration, assonance, etc.?

(iii) *Tropes:* Are there any obvious violations of, or departures from the linguistic code? Any deviant lexical collocations?

D. Cohesion and Context

This part includes the considerations of cohesion and context. By cohesion, we mean how one part of a text is joined to the other. This leads us to examine how sentences are connected in the internal organization of the text. With regard to context, the external relations of the text or part of it are considered. It means taking up the text as a discourse in which the author, the reader as also the text are related and share a common ground.

Now, we turn to the effect of some of these categories as pointed out by different linguists like Herbert Read, Fowler, Leech and Short, Quirk and Greenbaum et al.

Short sentences: These give the impression of speed and therefore are best used in action.

Long sentences: These indicate thinking and seriousness.

Complex sentences: These are best suited to express complex ideas and feelings. They afford variety, shift emphasis and help elaboration.

Antithetical sentences: These effectively express contrasting ideas and add point and vivacity. If abused, these can also make description tedious and artificial. They also balance two opposite ideas.

Anticipatory constituents: bring an element of suspense into the syntax.

Periodic sentence structure: builds suspense, adds dramatic quality to the writing, and is effective device for end-focus.

Parataxis: is associated with simple and naive narration.

Wh- questions: used for seeking new information.

Yes or no questions: allow little or no freedom to reply.

Modality: is the grammar of explicit comment, the means by which people express their degree of commitment to the truth of the proposition they utter, and their desirability, or otherwise of the states of affairs referred to.

Non-finite clauses: i.e. clauses with infinitive with to, infinitive without to, ing-partciple are marks of a careful style. They serve the purpose of compression and compactness. If applied indiscriminately, they make the writing ambiguous.

Emotive Emphasis: depends on the emphasis given by information, focus and theme. The language also provides means of giving a unit purely emotional emphasis. Exclamations, expletives, intensifiers, including the general clause emphasisers, such as, actually, really, indeed are included.

Here is an attempt at textural analysis of some lines taken from Anita Desai's novel *Voices in the City* (Ch. 1) according to the categories formulated by Leech and Short and the analytical model of M. Chakranarayan.

Text:

> The train began to pant, as though in preparation for a battle, sending jets of white steam violently into the night sky, and on the platform people loitered in various attitudes of nervousness, impatience and regret, turning now and then to the lights at the head of the platform, waiting for them to change (1). No one ever betrayed reluctance for them to do so except, perhaps, the latecomers pounding along with baggage wobbling and disintegrating on the seemingly hopeless search for the right carriage (2). 'I'm sorry, now, to leave,' Arun reflected (3). He was one of those who never disclosed nervousness or impatience, lounged over a cigarette as though he were relaxing on a terrace at night-fall (4). So it seemed to the red-shirted coolies, the tea-vendors and the stationmaster in grimy white, all stained with the sweat of haste and overwork, but Nirode, casting at him a glance made sly by envy, saw the tautness in the young man's body, and saw how his eyes shone (5). He threw away his cigarette and immediately lit another (6). 'Liar,' he said (7). 'You're itching to start' (8). Arun laughed (9). He moved, and from his movement one could see how right Nirode was (10). The man was like a bird poised on the roof's edge for flight, each feather alert and trained for it, vivid in this moment of gigantic expectation (11). He was alight with eagerness (12). Yet he laughed, stammered, 'No, it's not a moment for decisions' (13). I can't decide now what I'd most like to happen. . . (14). *Total words: 259*

The novel begins with a scene at the busy railway platform of Howrah. The train is about to leave, and Arun and Nirode, two brothers await the moment. Arun is leaving by the train, and Nirode who has come to see him off is envious of his brother's lot. Arun poses to be relaxed, but Nirode knows that he is eager to start a new life in the distant land. Both find the moment of separation difficult.

General observations: The passage abounds in polysyllabic words. Most of the abstract nouns are polysyllabic. The vocabulary is formal, and includes words of emotive and associative connotations. The passage shows idiomatic use of language. A few compound words are included, as for example *tea-vendors, night-fall, red-shirted.*

Nouns: Two proper nouns introduce the two characters. Almost equal number of concrete and abstract nouns has been included, but the abstract nouns are foregrounded, as they refer to the mental states of the people at the platform, and that of the protagonists. Many of these abstract nouns have negative connotations *i.e. nervousness, impatience, regret, battle, reluctance, haste, over-work, envy, tautness.* Only one abstract noun refers to happy state—*expectation.* The rest are neutral referring to mental processes and perceptions.

Adjectives: Here adjectives refer to both physical and psychological states. To match the nouns with negative connotations, most of the adjectives too have negative implications. Adjectives coupled with abstract nouns, heighten the effect of the unseen mental activity going on in the mind of the protagonists.

Verbs: To match the abstract nouns and adjectives denoting emotive and psychological states and adverbs of negative connotations, verbs mostly intransitive in nature have been included, *viz., pounding, wobbling, disintegrating, reflected* etc.

Adverbs: Of manner mostly with negative connotations predominate, e.g. *seemingly, unashamedly, heartbrokenly, dryly.*

Grammatical Categories

Average sentence length is 17.85 words. Only six short sentences of direct speech are included, the rest are all declarative sentences. Sentences are mostly long, only those stating direct speech are the shortest. Complexity is due to subordination and coordination both, but more due to the nature of subordinators, such as: *as though,* is compound subordinator, (Quirk and Greenbaum 292), *but* (3) and *yet* (2) denoting contrast. Complexity in sentence structure suggests complexity in ideas. The passage deals more with hidden psychological details than with overt physical surroundings.

Figures of Speech

The train began to pant and *waiting wheels* are both examples of *personification,* the train has been treated as animate, something which signifies journey into the future, symbolizing locomotion, uncertainty and promise.

Quasi-simile
As though in preparation for a battle (sent. 1).
As though he were relaxing on a terrace (sent.4).

The above analogies intensify the impression of a mind which constantly tries to analyze and evaluate men and objects around it. The fact that the objective and the subjective are inseparable is strengthened by these statements.

Simile: The man *was like a bird poised* on the roof's edge for *flight,* each *feather* alert and trained for it, vivid in this moment of gigantic expectation. He was alight with eagerness. (Sentences 11 and 12). Bird imagery is frequent in the works of Anita Desai. Birds denote nature, flights into fancy and freedom. The epithets used aptly describe Arun's preparation and expectations.

Parenthesis: It occurs once in these fourteen lines. It gives an impression of after-thought in sentence (1).

Context: The passage is a third person narration, containing a commentary on the scene at the railway platform. The focus of attention are two men—Arun and Nirode. In fact, it is Nirode's consciousness which controls the passage. The implicit uncertainty, nervousness, impatience and conflict in Nirode's temperament are made explicit through his interaction with his brother and surroundings. Even though third and fourth paragraphs speak of Arun, it is an interpretation of Nirode's consciousness. The passage is, in fact, a long metaphor, hinting at the contrasts and contradictions inherent in his character.

Cohesion: Paragraph arrangement is conspicuous in the passage. The first paragraph describes the train, ready to leave; in subjective terms. The middle lines narrate the attitude and reactions of the two brothers. Arun's journey by train is compared to the flight of a bird, thus the train serves as a referential link between the sentences and paragraphs. It also serves as a backdrop of palpable world for the mental activity in the forefront.

Analysis:

M. Chakranarayan points out the following anomalies:

Sentence 1

The train began *to pant* as though in preparation for a *battle.* (The word 'pant' suggests gasping for breath. Can a breathless entity be prepared for battle?)

Sending jets of *white* steam *violently. (white* is the colour of truce, of peace, here it is coupled with *violence.)*

On the platform people *loitered* in various attitudes of nervousness, impatience and regret. *(Loitered* suggests passing time indolently, here it is contrasted with attitude of nervousness, impatience and regret.)

Sentence 3

'I'm sorry, now, to leave,' Arun reflected.

('now,' enclosed within two commas hints that Arun is sorry at the prospect of leaving in the present time reference, the idea was welcome to him in the past.

Sentence 4

He (Arun) was one of those who *never disclosed* nervousness or impatience. (A contrast between appearance and reality.)

Sentence 6

Nirode *threw away* his cigarette and *immediately* lit another, which shows his nervousness.

Sentence 11

The man was like a bird poised on the roof's edge for *flight*, each feather *alert* and trained for it, vivid in this moment for *gigantic expectation.*

Assessment

The sentences analyzed show the writer's mastery over the choice of appropriate words to convey the inner landscape of characters. Desai prefers simple mixture of Saxon and Latin words. Although writing about human psyche she uses more concrete nouns than abstract ones. For vividness and visibility she includes adjectives, referring to physical and psychological states. The narrative voice is projected in evaluative epithets. A large number of adverbs of time, place, direction and degree give her writing a palpable quality—and the adverbs of manner throw light on the personality of the character, so as to render its total image for immediate apprehension. A judicious use of disjuncts, adjuncts and conjuncts clarifies the contrasts and juxtapositions of which her writing is full. A balanced use of transitive and intransitive verbs adds speed to the progression of images, which are created in order to dramatize an inner conflict and symbolize it objectively through a situation or object. The transitive verbs give the reader an impression of movement and activity and thus add liveliness to the description.

Desai prefers complex sentences to simple ones. The complexity arises due to both subordination and coordination. Desai favours non-finite clauses, *i.e.,* infinitive with to, infinitive without to, ing-participle and ed- participle. The use of non-finite clauses is a mark of careful writing. These clauses result in compactness and hence aid fluent reading. Relative clauses and adverb clauses are frequently used for pre-modification and post-modification. Anticipatory clauses, also frequently used, serve the purpose of orientation and add suspense to the writing.

Metaphors and similes, personification, pathetic fallacy, alliteration and assonance are very common, but the towering figure employed by Desai is that of irony which serves as the leitmotif in almost all her writings. A strong liking for imagery needs to be mentioned here. Birds are symbolically very prominent in *Voices in the City*. Parataxis, ellipsis and parenthesis are other devices employed freely. They save the narration from being formal and keep the naturalistic view of expression. Parentheses are termed to show intimacy with the readers.

For cohesion, she resorts to lexical repetition, the use of pronouns and definite article. She charts out the lexical items and stylistic details, insisting that the reader should be wary of not only what is put in words but also that which is implicit. Further, there is strong unifying link between paragraphs. The material is organized in a careful manner. The sentences are placed logically and sequentially. For example, *Voices in the City,* begins with a general comment on the train. The ending paragraph in the passage also has a comment on the general activities associated with the train in addition to the parting of the two brothers, which has been foregrounded in the middle part. Desai's majestic grip of playing with language and thoughts is subtle and appreciable.

Works Cited

Desai, Anita. *Voices in the City.* New Delhi: Orient Paperback, 1965.

Fowler, Roger, ed. *Essays on Style and Language.* London: University College, 1967.

Leech, Geoffrey N. & Michael H. Short. *Style in Fiction.* London: Longman. 1981

Lodge, David, *Language in Fiction.* New York: Columbia University Press, 1967.

Mohini Chakranarayan. *Style Studies in Anita Desai.* New Delhi: Atlantic, 2000.

Quirk, R. and S. Greenbaum. *A University Grammar of English.* London: Longman, 1973.

Novel as Discourse: A Stylistic Reading of R.K. Narayan's *The Guide*

S.L. PAUL

The term discourse came into prominence with the Russian Formalists, more particularly with Mikhail Bakhtin. Normally, a discourse means a speech, a lecture, a sermon or a talk but in critical parlance it eventually came to mean a speech or a writing, a book or a text without a centre, or subject, or a privileged reference. In Derrida, it receives a new status in the abandonment of any reference to the origin, i.e., *arche* and the end, i.e., *telos*. Nor should it refer to all the analogues for the centre—subject and substance, essence and existence, God and Man. It means that a discourse, a speech or a writing, has no underpinning, either theological or metaphysical. Discourse is thus what is open to sight or lets itself be seen. The original Greek meaning of logos is also discourse, that which shows itself or lets itself seen as it is. Language in this sense is a phenomenon, as it discards all preconceived logical or epistemological constructions and seeks to examine and describe the phenomena as they show themselves.

The application of this phenomenological method in the analysis of human beings in R.K. Narayan's world of Malgudi, especially with reference to *The Guide*, discloses, first of all, the foundational experience of being-in-the-world. Men in Narayan emerge in a world of on-going concerns and initially discover themselves in their engagement in practical and personal projects. The world is not an extended substance or an objective container into which they live. The world, existentially understood, is a field of region of human concern which is never disclosed independent of this concern. Human reality in Narayan's novels is found in a self-world correlation, which underlines all concrete participation and engagement. Even Vasu in The Man-Eater of Malgudi takes no time to get entangled in the affairs of Natraj, though he is no socialized being in any sense of the word.

Herein lies the source of comedy in Narayan, as his characters in their varied concerns and in their equally varied voices form what Bakhtin called a carnival. Raju's world is the world he shares with others. Human beings in Narayan are essentially communal and the language they speak is chatter, rather than speech proper. An attempt is made in the present paper to study *The Guide* as an illustration of novel as discourse, involving Narayan's world-view as communal, as it shows itself in human involvement and since this involvement is inauthentic, it produces comedy, even by extending the limits of comedy to the edge of parodying and travestying of the traditional myth of becoming of the saint and of the waiting for the Mahatma.

Nevertheless, the purpose of parodying-travestying is not negative. It has never been the case even with the epics. Homer himself wrote a comic epic in *Margites* and Milton conceived of Satan as a mock-heroic figure. English novels of Fielding and Sterne began with the comic. Shakespeare's grimmest tragedy is fraught with the comic in its depiction of follies. In all these cases, the purpose of laughter has been to arouse mankind to authentic existence. It is specifically the case with *The Guide*. It is dialogic in form. As the novel opens, we find Raju sitting on the slab of a ruined temple outside the village Mangal. He has been sitting there for quite sometime, after his release from the prison two days ago. He had walked to this place, as he had nowhere else to go. He wanted to be away from his own people, after serving two years in the prison.

But while sitting thus alone, Raju was troubled because there was no human soul to talk to. Man, as Narayan finds, is essentially communal. The community of human beings is a pervasive phenomenon, which shows itself in man's experience of aloneness, as assuredly as in his experience, of being-with-others. Aloneness is a deficient mode of being-with-others. Raju experiences aloneness, only as a privation of an original communal relatedness. But for the most part, he exists in the inauthentic mode. That is why his troubles begin ever and anon. Indeed, he says, in the first chapter: "My troubles would not have started (Raju said in the course of narrating his life story to Velan at a later stage) but for Rosie."

But could this awareness stop him from avoiding another entanglement with Velan and with the villagers of Mangal? When he saw a villager crossing the river-bed and coming toward the temple, he felt relieved of his aloneness. Narayan in the opening sentence of the novel expresses Raju's sense of relief: "Raju welcomed the intrusion—something to relieve his loneliness of the place."

And when the villager, Velan by name, looked at him reverentially, as the latter was found sitting in the temple cross-legged, Raju felt amused and embarrassed. He wanted to break the ice, and talk to Velan. He asked, "Where are you from?" dreading lest the other should turn around and ask the same question. However, the man replied, "I am from Mangal" and then Velan, unasked, started his rambling talk, that he had been to his daughter's place, married to the son of her sister and so on.

The novel as a whole is oriented to the language of talk, as Eliot put it in Prufrock: "Women come and go/ Talking of Michelangelo." What Eliot meant was that women in the poem talk, not speak, i.e., they indulged in meaningless and idle talk. Narayan would say that an accurate account of what is communicated between the speaker and the listener must be based on the existential situation rather than purely linguistic or even purely logical solution, that is, who is saying it, under which conditions, to whom it is said, the personality of the hearer and the speaker. Hence, the basis of language is neither grammar nor logic, but talk, talk as opposed to speech, or special as phenomenon, as Derrida would have it, having no privileged subject behind it. For instance, soon after coming out of the prison, Raju got himself shaved. The barber, talkative as ever, asked Raju: "Coming out, I suppose?" and repeated, as he did not receive the reply: "Just coming out?" Out of curiosity, Raju asked: "How do you know?" In reply, the barber said that he has spent twenty years shaving people here. It was followed by his rambling information regarding his profession and his experience of judging criminal—big or small—by face-reading.

Narayan uses talk because it is essentially characteristic of human beings inter-relating each other, intrigued, of course, by the commerce of things in the world and many subtle relations with other humans. To maintain, as Narayan does, such an activity or mode of existence, on the basis of language, has tremendous consequences for any theory of language. If Narayan is correct, then any formal analysis of language is, in principle, inadequate. Furthermore, if his account is correct, the locus of truth must be shifted from proposition to the existential basis of such proposition. The classic example of this is when Raju talks to Velan's half-wit brother in order to convey his message, "Tell your brother immediately, wherever he may be, unless they are good, I'll never eat."

The boy, even if he were not a half-wit, would have felt bewildered, for the villagers were fighting to eat, and here was the Swami who wished not to eat. The boy asked, "Eat what?" He was rather puzzled. Raju again said: "Say that I'll not eat. Don't ask what. I'll not eat till they are good." The boy again felt puzzled and asked: "Good? Where?" as if it were a place name. Narayan intervened to say: "This was frankly beyond the comprehension of the boy. . . .He could not connect the fight and this man's food."

The meaning of a particular expression could not be analyzed merely by consideration of the logical and grammatical properties of that particular sentence. The boy, Velan's brother, felt so terrified over what the Swami said (otherwise a well-ordered expression) that he wanted only to be released. He felt that the man might eat him up. And when he ran into villagers to blurt out the message, he said: "The Swami, the Swami, doesn't want food any more. Don't take any food to him." Asked why, he said: "Because it does not rain." He added suddenly, recollecting the Swami's mention of the fight: "No fight," he says. Again, he remembered what the Swami said: "He wants no food until it is all right." It is this last that Velan and other villagers felt intoned to and asked the boy to tell them exactly what the Swami said. The boy deliberated for a moment and said: "Tell your brother not to bring any food. I won't eat. If I don't eat, it'll be all right; and then everything will be all right."

It is not the logic or grammar of language which is important here, but who is spoken to and under what conditions. The villagers were facing the worst of the dry spell. They were fighting against the hoarders. Their animals were beginning to die. Before they could realize the meaning of what the boy said, one of the villagers stated: "Mangal is a blessed country to have a man like the Swami in our midst. No bad thing will come to us as long as he is with us. He is like the Mahatma. When Mahatma Gandhi went without food, how many things happened in India," and then the fellow referred to Mahatma Gandhi observing fast for twenty-one days and since this man was like that and, if he fasts, there will be rain. In no time, the whole village was astir.

This is what Bakhtin would call 'polyphonic,' many-voiced discourse, expressing different positions set in play without being placed under and judged by a totalizing authorial discourse. He found this kind of fiction while working on Dostoevsky. Later he came to think that this was not a unique discovery of Dostoevsky, but an inherent characteristic of the novel as a literary form—one he traced back to its origin in the parodying-travestying genres of classical and medieval cultures, i.e., in the form of the carnival.

Narayan was no theorist of the novel, but he saw to it that there are left no traces of the metaphysical in the discourse, albeit the dialogic. The dialogic, however, is not simply having dialogues between persons. That has always been the case with drama. Besides, the play of voices as part of any dramatic discourse, the dialogue as Bakhtin conceived it, was reinforced by the parodying and travestying, i.e., the given utterance may be, not just the representation of something in the world but also a representation of another speech-act about that thing. The boy, who reported Raju's utterances made a travesty, not intentionally of what the Swami said. It was a kind of doubly-oriented discourse. As a corollary, a novel like *The Guide* does more justice to language than the canonical genres—epic, lyric and tragedy, privileged by orthodox poetics,—a capacity it derives from the parodying-travestying.

Narayan's use of language as talk reveals this aspect of the parodic, because he thinks that when the boy heard Raju, the former heard a message, but when he came to report, the same or at least a part of it, he left behind of what occurred in the communication. Instead, he added something of his own, in terms of supplementarity, as Derrida would say, having scandalous implications in French. Language, of course, is communication. But we do not hear or read words. The hearer or reader contributes his own talk. This means, he involves himself, not as a viewer of words on the page, but as a fellow human being for whom the spoken words excite an existential response. Moreover, when the message is delivered, the speaker always keeps something of his message ambiguous—it cannot be exposed, cannot be made to resonate, can be seen but not heard, as in the word *differance*, the reader and the receiver of the message thus differ and defer, differing, deferring.

Raju said that he would not eat, but added, "till they are 'good'." He twice uttered that word in order to emphasize that if they continued their fight, the police might come upon the scene, and he did not want to be recognized as a jail-bird, by any chance. Of course, Raju also said that they should not fight, but before the boy could rehearse the message, Raju put in the word 'good.' This contributed to the boy's confusion. And when he added to the inquiry why would the Swami not eat, he said, "Because, because it doesn't rain." The villagers could see the logic—penance for appeasing rain-gods.

Narayan's main point is that truth does not reside in the purely formal or logical characteristic of proposition. It, however, does not mean that one cannot communicate with words. Raju's message, itself ambiguous, was interpreted in an entirely opposite manner from what it was intended. It was because he was far behind the possibilities. He had been in his fallen state right from the beginning of his life. He became what the time, space and circumstances made him. His house and his father's shop were closer to the Railway station and so on. And when one day Marco (named by Raju) came with Rosie, his wife. Raju turned a tourist guide, guiding Marco and then Rosie. When jailed for forgery, he started guiding prisoners. And finally, the guide in him took on a new avatar by assuming *swamihood*, the spiritual guide, by proxy.

The essence of Raju thus is his existence, i.e., the world existentially understood is the field of his concern which is never disclosed independent of this concern. Raju takes on all these forms of guiding as his profession. In fact, he, during his confession, says that he too would have grown up like most young men but for his tendency to get involved, in whatever is, on hand. The parodying-travestying is occasioned by his tendency to get involved in whatever is on-hand, not realizing whether this relationship would help or harm him. When he finds Velan looking reverentially at him, he strokes his chin to ascertain whether a saintly beard has grown up, because he got himself shaved only two days back. But he does not realize that he was sitting in the backdrop of a temple. He realizes how harmful this involvement has been when he is trapped in his own devices.

Narayan uses parody in showing that saints are not born but become, under compulsions, and these compulsions and circumstances are part of their factuality and possibility. Between the two, however, lies the region of their fallenness. In Raju, this fallenness finds its trenchant expression in his gossip, his curiosity, his ambiguity. He, for one, takes no time, to indulge in gossip—idle chatter, to be precise. After having a bitter taste of his involvement with Rosie, Raju again indulges in idle talk with Velan, when the latter seeks his guidance regarding his sister's affair.

"I have a problem, Sir," said the man. Raju nodded his head and added, "So has everyone, in a sudden access of pontificality." Raju felt like an actor. Now the appropriate sentence for the above expression, he thought, is: "If you show me a person without a problem, then I'll show you the perfect world. Do you know what the great Buddha said?" And he related the story. He felt he was attaining the stature of a saint. Gossip is an unauthentic modification of speech, which Raju has acquired the skill to use, simply repeating the accepted, everyday, conventional, and shallow clichés. No decisive content is communicated, because gossip is concerned only with situations of commonplaces which reflect Raju's restricted world-horizon.

He is also curious to know how his clichés affect his listeners, as for example, in inviting the boy to know the ongoing fight in the village, out of his fears, not for the purpose of authentic understanding. Curiosity, for him, is at times, simply to engage in pursuits which will provide him with momentary diversion, as is the case with idle talk. Ambiguity is the lack of comprehension on his part and singleness of purpose, as when in order to get out of the trap of observing the fast, he decided to confess that he was no saint, and to this end told the whole story of his life from the beginning, but the confession was so long that it perhaps drugged Velan to sleep. On waking, as against Raju's expectation, that he would be kicked out, as unholy, Velan thumped his chest and said that all that the Swami told him would lie buried in his heart. Raju was left with no choice but to go through the fast in order, as he said, to give the poor devil a chance. Raju's last remarks also remained ambiguous as his gesture of sagging down in the bed of the river. He said, "Velan, it is raining in the hills."

Narayan's, like Bakhtin's, emphasis is not on the formal aspect of language. Language and words make sense only in communication, directed towards another. The sign in Narayan is not, as Saussure argued, a stable unit, but an active component of speech in a social context. The sign, as Raju gave to the half-wit brother of Velan, was a site for struggle and contradiction, since social conditions are amorphous and heterogeneous, ridden with conflicting interests. The villagers of Mangal had different interests in Swami's gesture, in not eating, and therefore they interpreted the message in their own terms, by adding that the Swami would not eat till it rained.

Thus, the village Mangal becomes a carnival, a site of laughter. But there is no object of laughter, because villagers are both spectators and participants. Who is the object of laughter—Raju or the villagers? The carnival is thus subversive. Carnival logic underlines the non-academic discourse, because it resists the academic repression of ambivalence. The reading of *The Guide* in terms of 'poetics' might do an injustice to its richness. That is why Narayan also resorted to the dialogic, an interplay of many voices and sounds, none of which is repressed, leading to unfinalisability of *The Guide*.

Work Cited

Narayan, R.K. *The Guide*. Mysore: The Indian Thought Publications, 1958, Reprint 1985.

English Becomes 'Native' in Arundhati Roy's *The God of Small Things*

URMIL HOODA

Some two thousand years before the birth of Christ is the approximate date of the beginning of Indian literature in Sanskrit, when it was decided that the verbal transmission of invaluable treatises and profound knowledge was an unsafe mode of imparting knowledge. So, the *Vedas* were written. The epics like the *Mahabharata* and the *Ramayana* were still passed on verbally for centuries to the next generation before being penned down.

In our country, apart from twenty-two official languages, there are more than 1600 dialects, and all languages and dialects are almost equally enriched with epics, written or unwritten. It is this extra emphasis on verbal mode of transmission of culture which provided the right environment for so many 'tongues' to grow. It is not that every language originated here, but, whoever came to this immensely resourceful land for what-so-ever reason, from the Aryans to the Tibetans, they only added their shade to the enormously rich culture of this soil.

Now moving on to our language of interest, the arrival of the English people in this subcontinent goes back to 1608 when Captain William Hawkins landed in the Court of Emperor Jahangir and established the East India Company. The history of English language starts in 1835 with the Governor General William Bentinck agreeing to Lord Thomas Babington Macaulay's Minutes recommending English to be both *lingua franca* as well as the medium of education. It is not that it was only imposed by the colonizers, there was also another necessity to get acquainted with the language. Indians wanted to project their thoughts on freedom and need of independence and also wanted to get familiar with the shelves full of western books and ideas full of inventions. During the two world wars, English became important as the language of communication with the outer world, particularly the West. Still, till Independence, only a limited creamy layer was acquainted with the language. The three pillars of the Indian novel in English, viz., Mulk Raj Anand, R.K. Narayan and Raja Rao, had started writing, even then it was only in the 1960s that the number of writers increased and in the nineties, both the number and the output increased.

Confining myself to my writer of interest, I want to establish two facts here; first, that English was a foreign language and within an incredibly small span the writers like the one under the scan now, Arundhati Roy, have contributed a lot in simplifying it and making it 'native' by blending it with typical Indian spices, and secondly, the method Roy adopts to achieve that aim is by jotting down a story with all the typical ancient tradition of story- telling.

Whether it was to infuse Indian consciousness into English or to make English pliant for the Indian tongue, or both, Arundhati Roy has experimented a lot with the form and semantics of the language. In spite of a few adverse comments back home, *The God of Small Things* was bestowed the 1997 Booker prize which was clearly an appreciation of her attempt to ignore the English literary tradition. But actually her work carries the baton of the Indian literature and tradition ahead.

The beginning of the novel with an epigraph from John Berger, "Never again will a single story be told as though it's the only one," is a clear indication that her motto is to narrate a story in English using all the means generally implied in verbal story-writing. She was blamed for wrongly getting applauded for the work is merely the outcome of a person well-acquainted with the functions of a computer. But the fact, which I could sense, is that she has used the printing option only to introduce the oral mode.

When a reader is going through *The God of Small Things*, it does not seem that he is simply going though the work. Instead, the feeling of an imaginary narrator dominates as he turns the pages. To be more precise, wherever the italics are used, it is an indication that the voice of the narrator has come down to the level of a whisper. The first few lines to be italicized are the words of a priest on the funeral of Sophie Mol:

> The sad priests' voices muffled by mud and wood.
> *We entrust into thy hands, most merciful Father,*
> *The soul of this our child departed,*
> *And we commit her body to the ground,*
> *Earth to earth, ashes to ashes, dust to dust.* (7)
> The letters Baby Kochamma writes to her father (25), "'*It is a far, far better thing that I do, than I have ever done,*' she would say to herself sadly" (61).

Roy has used the mode of changing printing blocks to bring in the element of oral transmission into her work. Roy has used Italics to be taken as the slowing down of story-teller to the level of whispering and sudden bold is the sudden rising of the pitch where the sub-consciousness of the reader takes those words as loud words and whispers, because of their extra emphasis, which attracts the sight more, and the lighter words, where you stress more; not only the narrator's voice whispers down in italics words, but it is raised or extra-emphasized also, like in any story telling, which is indicated by the bold letters.

> 'Estha,' Ammu said affectionately, 'when someone says How d'you do? You're supposed to say How d'you do? Back. Not "Fine, thank you." Come on, say How do YOU do?' (145)

This seems an apt example of how language could be distorted to the extent of absurdity, if we take these words on the basis of aesthetics. But, if any reader would try to speak out these words exactly as they are written, we find that he need not have a strong imagination to almost feel Ammu's face with its hard protruding jaw-line saying these words to a meek submissive introvert Estha. It all comes out alive in front of the reader's eyes. The playing with the words and printing blocks only helps Roy to say the story than to let others read it.

Roy does not stop here only. She goes much ahead and her narrators being children, she uses their sub-conscious and unconscious to be reflected on the pages of the work. The language moves with the thoughts of the children breaking all rules of the language for the chief aim is to speak it out as she wants than letting others to read as they want.

By clubbing together the words, or reversing the order of the words, or by using hyphenated words, or by using phrases as full sentences, she is actually bringing the traditional element of oral transmission into the English novel. To make reader feel that she is telling the story, instead that the reader is reading it, she has used these techniques to declare English to be very much 'native' than a foreign language.

I would quote a few examples stating how those grammatically incorrect sentences, when spoken, words create a sort of magical imagery which just plainly printed words never could. First, there is a talk about Mammachi's head regularly receiving beatings from Pappachi. And Roy explains it so forcefully, like she is telling the story, through those incomplete or grammatically incorrect sentences. Roy says: "On her scalp, carefully hidden by her scanty hair, Mammachi had raised, crescent-shaped ridges. Scars of old beatings from an old marriage. Her brass vase scars" (166).

Her clubbing together of words or unnecessary breaking of words is again another liberty with the language to keep her story-telling going. Secondly, she herself becomes a child, when she tells about Sophia Mol, another child. Roy says:

> Bluegrayblue eyes snapped open.
> A Wake
> A Live
> A Lert (238)

The clubbing together of words (Bluegrayblue) is to show the detail of Sophie's each eye minutely. And further breaking of the words (Awake, Alive and Alert), on print, show no difference but when spoken, they do make an incredible effect on the listener. In her work, Roy does not forget her primary target of story-telling for which she sidelines all grammar rules and takes all liberty with the language to emphasize its 'Nativity.'

To quote further, when K.N.M. Pillai sees Estha and Rahel stepping through the temple gateway, he, "in his piping voice" (237) shows amazement that both are still interested in Kathak dance, and he appreciates and further says, "Goodgood. Very good" (237) which surely is grammatically incorrect, but when we imagine the way in which Pillai might have uttered, the point becomes clear, for the first two 'good' would be like one word and then further emphasis with another good prefixed with 'very.'

Secondly, when Vellya Paapen goes to Mammachi with his stone eye in his hand, he is "torn between Loyalty and Love" (255), where Roy has projected both the emotions as living beings, and further, "Terror" holds Vellya where again the first letter of this emotion also is capital. And this is how the language is simplified for the natives without compromising its effect.

The world, seen through the eyes of two zygotic-twins, Estha and Rahel, has been described by Roy in a language which takes full liberty with the grammar, semantics, tectonics etc. Thus, she uses grammatically wrong and incomplete sentences, ignores punctuation, clubbing and distorting words as also reversing their order. There is also, in her novel, repetition of words, use of bold alphabets within a word etc., which makes the language very much 'local.' These techniques were implied only to free the language from the shackles of 'Oxford' rules and twisting, smashing and squeezing it to fit on the tongue of her characters. This subversion by Roy from the trodden path is a forceful effort to make the language more native, be it the abundant use of the words from Hindi and Malayalam like Namaste (139), Naale (340), Keto (70) Valerey (70), Ividay (71), etc. or the use of italics and bold letters which are a part of her storytelling only.

The literary discourse always differs from verbal communication; when the story comes through pen, it undergoes the process of repetitive writing, cautious composition, much revision and proof-reading before publication, but when it comes through tongue, it has to have repetitions and elisions, high-pitched emphasizing and low-pitched whispering, unnecessary elaboration and necessary interpretations. And here lies the strength of Roy when she is mixing these two totally different mediums and what comes out would be something like *The God of Small Things* only where it is on paper but all the play with the type-case is to make it look like recitation. When you read out this text to yourself aloud, you listen to the novel rather than read it. Only then you enjoy the dialogues. Like our epics it could be enjoyed by a person from any age group. Taking the legacy-baton of Indian writing in English from such stalwarts as Raja Rao, Mulk Raj Anand and R.K. Narayan, Roy has undoubtedly opened the horizons of Indian English by simplifying and localizing it.

Work Cited

Roy, Arundhati. *The God of Small Things* New Delhi: IndiaInk, 1997.

A Linguistic Appraisal of Rohinton Mistry's *Such a Long Journey*

MEENAKSHI

Rohinton Mistry is a widely acclaimed writer of Indian English fiction. He occupies a significant position among the writers of Indian Diaspora. A glowing star in the galaxy that contains luminaries such as V.S. Naipaul, Salman Rushdie, Amitav Ghosh, Shashi Tharoor, Vikram Seth, to mention a few, Rohinton Mistry has drawn the attention of the world as an absorbing writer of human experiences. Rohinton Mistry is also famous as a Parsi writer and is grouped along with Bapsi Sidhwa, Dina Mehta, Keki Daruwalla and Boman Desai. His scholarly insight into the Zoroastrian faith as well as his objective detachment and capacity for self-analysis enabled him to be regarded as an authentic Parsi writer of his time. An India-born novelist settled in Canada, Rohinton Mistry has remarkable capacity for capturing the crowded, throbbing life of India.

Rohinton Mistry as a fiction writer occupies an important place in Indian writing in English. Right from his first offering titled *Tales from Firozsha Baag*, it had become clear that Indian English fiction had got a very talented writer. Being based in Canada does not affect the depth of his insight into the Indian reality. Mistry is a fine story-teller, an absorbing writer of human experience and its complexities, for fictionalizing which he occasionally uses postmodernist technique and fantasy that shape his fictional universe.

In *Such a Long Journey*, the main plot focuses on the life of Gustad Noble, who is an ordinary bank clerk living in the Parsi housing complex Khodadad building in Bombay, now Mumbai. The major events of the history of post-independence India have been included in the main plot. The novel is set again the backdrop of Indo-Pak war and the birth of Bangladesh. As the story advances, conflict envelopes the life of Gustad Noble and his family. His son Sohrab betrays him of his dream by refusing to enroll himself as an IIT student. His daughter's illness and sudden disappearance of his intimate friend Major Bilimoria and at last his friend Dinshawji's death are some of the tensions in his life.

Miss Kutpitia, Tehmul Langda and Dinshawji are some other characters who play significant roles. There is also the pavement artist and Gulam Muhammad who make their present felt. Dr. Paymaster and Peerbhoy Paanwala lend an interesting touch to the story. The main-plot, however, is centred around the Nagarwala case, one of the scandals of the Indira Gandhi era. Major Bilimoria is crafted in the image of Nagarwala. He finally dies and his death leaves behind a mystery as it happened in reality. But in the meanwhile, Gustad has to pass through harrowing times. The purpose of the writer is to show the callousness with which the politicians play on the chessboard of politics without any regard for the common man.

In this, Mistry comes out as a very successful author and one of the major factors contributing to his success is the command of English language. He has a huge vocabulary from which he draws liberally to make his narrative accurate and comprehensive. He has the knack for expressing complex feelings. He has an observant eye; nothing goes unnoticed, as for example, when in the following lines, Mistry describes Gustad's agony at Sohrab's dismissive attitude towards him as the son rejects father's advice to join an engineering college: "Gustad gave the forms to Sohrab, and told him to count the number of places he had been to for a worthless, ungrateful boy, the number of time she touched his forehead and folded his hands and said 'sir' and 'madam' and 'please' and 'thank you very much.'" (94).

The sixth chapter ends with a defiant Sohrab throwing the scholarship application forms which his father had laboriously procured, into the dustbin and his mother retrieving the papers and putting them under the choolavati, where ironically, she has already put the green lemons, reminiscent of Dilnavaz's attempts to bring back the errant son, the Kutipitian way. The message that the author delivers is clear: the voodoo had failed.

Mistry's power of realistic portrayal comes out vividly in the following platform scene:

> The loudspeakers came alive with violent hissing and crackling, then a high-pitched hum. A hush descended upon the railway station. The tea-stall clatter ceased; the newsstand boys stopped calling; and the sudden quiet awakened the man on the bedding. He sat up with a start. Everyone waited for the voice from above to speak of deliverance. The hiss and crackle bore fruit: 'Checking checking checking. One two three four. Checking. *Ek do teen chaar.*' A painful whine. Then the voice again, hoarse and indistinct, the malfunctioning system devouring most of the words. The survivors emerged like grape seeds spat carelessly through the loudspeaker mesh: 'Passengers are req . . . to vacate the plat . . . and wait in the . . . trains arrive . . . at which time . . . ssengers with tickets may . . . platforms.' (257).

The half-formed words tell quite a realistic tale of the inaudible announcements—a common experience on railway platforms across India.

Mistry has a superb command of words. He can use words to evoke any kind of mood or atmosphere. In the following passage, Mistry shows his skill in imparting a sublime, spiritual experience in poetic language:

> The prayers filled the dark room slowly. Slowly, the prayer sound was the dark room. And before he was aware of it, Gustad was under its gentle spell. He forgot the time, forgot Alamai, forgot Nusli. He listened to the music, the song in a language which he did not understand, but which was wondrously soothing. All his life he had uttered by rote the words of this dead language, comprehending not one of them while mouthing his prayers. But tonight, in the *dustoorji*'s soft and gentle music, the words were alive; tonight he came closer than he ever had to understanding the ancient meanings.
>
> The *dustoorji* cantillated the verses of the ancient Avesta. And as the notes and syllables were intoned, they mingled with the sounds

> of night. Steadily, from the trees and bushes rose the voices of night and nature, and from all the lush vegetation that grew here on the hill, around the Tower of Silence. The murmurings of leaf-hoppers and tree-dwellers, winged and crawling, ascended Doongerwadi, up towards the Tower of Silence. Their murmurings blended with the sandalwood and *loban* and prayer music floating forth from the room with the oil lamp, and Gustad understood it all. (247-48)

The use of Free Indirect Discourse or FID is quite common in *Such a Long Journey*. Mistry mixes direct and indirect narration in a fascinating way when it comes to expressing series of actions in a compressed manner. The following description succeeds in depicting Gustad's stream of consciousness with focus on multiple images of childhood rushing through his mind:

> He saw a little boy holding his father's hand and walking timidly down these lanes. His father talking enthusiastically about antiques and curios, pointing, describing, explaining. The shopkeepers calling, Mr. Noble see this vase, you will like it, Mr. Noble, very rare plate, saving it just for you, very cheap. And his father saying quietly in his ear, Listen to them, Gustad, listen to the thieves. And the little boy saying, Pappa, look, a Meccano set, such a big one. His father pleased, patting his head, saying, Yes, at least a number ten, sharp eyes you have, just like mine. Then his father bargaining, offering a preposterously low figure, haggling and dickering, are you crazy, walking away, come back sir, comeback, yes, walking back, no, go to hell, please take, honest price, in God's name, don't blaspheme, final figure, truthfully sahib, OK you thief—thus, the bargain sealed. (100)

The chain of thought requires a stimulus. Gustad remembers that as a child he had visited the Chor Bazar in the company of his father and had purchased a meccano set. This phrase 'meccano set' sets off a chain of thought that covers a very vital detail of the unfortunate bankruptcy which his father had to undergo, all because of his brother's alcoholism. Mistry also uses free indirect thought in the following conversation between Dilnavaz and Miss Kutpitia:

> 'You really think so?'
>
> 'Would I say it otherwise?'
>
> No, Miss Kutpitia would not say it unless she believed it. But what am I supposed to believe? 'OK, thank you. I will do it. And thank you also for giving the newspapers to Roshan. Her class now has highest collection for refugees.' (110)

Rohinton Mistry's use of language in *Such a Long Journey* has also a fine smattering of Indian, mainly Hindi and Gujarati words. Continuing in the tradition of Mulk Raj Anand who made necessary changes in English language in order to reveal Indian sensibility, Mistry excels in inserting maximum native words wherever he feels that translation of those words would fail to render Indian sensibility. It is possible to make a big list of Hindi and Gujarati words used in the novel. And the list may be divided into three parts. First, there are common Hindi words; then there is slang; and lastly, there is English translation of Hindi idioms as in the expression, 'turn tail and run.'

The novel has such Hindi expressions as 'Arre bhaiya,' 'Hindi-Chinese bhai bhai,' 'Humko kuch nahin maaloom' which at once reveal the Indian sensibility. There are the words such as 'chawal' and 'subjo' which are common Hindi words and Mistry rightly felt that these words are better than rice and vegetable for expressing the Indian scenario. Such kind of exposure can be called as 'Indianism' and the psychology of it. 'Goaswalla' is used instead of butcher, 'Seth' instead of 'Sir,' 'langra' instead of lame. For such words as 'basmati,' 'sappat,' 'goteloo,' there are hardly any English words. 'Gilly gilly gilly,' 'Chaalo,' 'Theek hai,' 'jaadu mantra' etc. are other examples of Hindi expressions which provide an Indian flavour to the English language used by Mistry.

Native words have been used in plenty. These include Hindi as well as Gujarati words, besides some Persian words connected with the Parsi culture. Here is a sample of Hindi words: "Theek hai, theek hai" (59), "Chaalo, time for drinks" (58), the chicken "did chee chee" (26) Gujarati abusive words: "ma-ka-pao" (99), "Goover-Ni-Gaan" (used to tease a colleague) (39). Nativism is also seen in the use of English words, the way semi-literate or even literate people do, as for example, "woman trouble" (36).

There are frequent uses of typical words such as 'meher-bani,' 'toba toba' which are blended with the English language. 'Dubbawalla,' 'Jaripuranawalla' are typical names indicating trades. Mistry even quotes some abusive terms used by ordinary people. For example, Dinshawji expresses his anger against Shiv Sena's campaign to change the English names of streets in Bombay: "'Why change the names? 'Saala sister fuckers! Hutatma Chowk!' He spat out the words disgustedly. 'What is wrong with Flora fountain?'" (73-74).

Mistry nativizes English with abandon. Apart from a large number of native words thrown into English text, he also uses Hindi structure in English, as in the expression: "Everything they would open up. In every gully-gootchy, *yaar*, in the dark, or under the stairs, what-what went on" (99). Every writer coins words wherever he or she feels the existing words inadequate for the purpose of expression of his ideas. Mistry refers to a certain 'gospel of beef' (26) used for his espousal of beef-eating, when he discusses non-vegetarianism with his friend Malcolm.

Cataloguing is a favourite device with a number of writers. Mistry also resorts to it to make his description realistic, as for example in the market scene: "Worthless junk lay side by side with valuable objects: chipped cups and saucers, Meissen ware, Sheffield cutlery, vases, brass lamps, Limoges porcelain, solder-repaired cooking utensils, ewers, wind-up gramophones with shining conical horns, silver trays, walking-sticks, weights and measures, cricket balls in varying stages of wear, refurbished cricket bats, umbrellas, crystal wineglasses" (101).

To bring variety into the description, Mistry changes the register sometimes, as for example, Dr. Paymaster narrates the events during the Bangladesh struggle in a medical register: " 'East Pakistan is suffering from a diarrhea of death,' he continued. 'Death is flowing there unchecked and the patient will soon be dehydrated.' [. . .] 'East Pakistan has been attacked by a strong virus from West Pakistan, too powerful for the Eastern immune system. And the world's biggest physician is doing nothing. Worse, Dr America is helping the virus. So what's the prescription? The Mukti Bahini guerillas?' He shook his head. 'Not strong enough medicine. Only the complete, intravenous injection of the Indian Army will defeat this virus.'" (164-65).

Mistry adds to the realistic effect in this novel through effective use of language as in case of Tehmul's habit of speaking non-stop, like 'Gustadpetitionpleasepetition. Signsignpetitionplease' (116) is a fine example even though Mistry is not the first practiser of this style. The spelling of the word 'Papa' has been changed to 'Pappa' to represent the pronunciation in a better way. If Dinshawji has some teeth missing because of which he cannot pronounce all words correctly, it is duly noted. The occasion is Roshan's birthday party at which he sings: "I wiss you. . ." (46). On the other hand, Gustad's drawl is also represented in the rhyme that he sings

> Gh-o-osts to right of them,
> Gho-o-osts to left of them,
> Gho-o-osts in front of them,
> Hungry and thirsty! (47)

Mistry uses imagery of different types. The bird image is used to describe hope in his heart: "He dropped his briefcase on the desk. The fledgling bits of hope he had been nurturing all day took wing. Like the sparrows that chirped in the compound's solitary tree, but flew away if the Landmaster backfired, Gustad's hope circled once over his head and departed" (186). Similarly, metaphorically speaking, Miss Kutpitia's cup is said to have been filled to overflowing by her nephew Farad while he was alive (283). The reader can easily guess with what the cup was filled; it was joy and peace.

Work Cited

Mistry, Rohinton. *Such a Long Journey*. London: Faber and Faber, 1991.

The Narrator's Voice in Aravind Adiga's *The White Tiger*

GEETA GOYAL

The present paper deals with the narrator's voice in Aravind Adiga's novel *The White Tiger*. Adiga presents an Indian citizen as the protagonist and narrator who claims to present the truth about his country to the readers through the experiences that he has undergone. In an unusual style by writing letter for over seven days and nights, Balram, the central character, narrates his life story in the first person. In order to catch the full flavour of Indian setting, the author has put the whole story in the mouth of a common man, a driver. Adiga's choice of the first person is determined by his intention to show the narrative authentic and true.

Born in Chennai on 23 October, 1974, Aravind Adiga grew up in Mangalore. After joining the *Time* magazine as a correspondent, he travelled throughout India, particularly in Uttar Pradesh and Bihar where he got the opportunity to see a lot of rural life. Through his epoch making debut novel *The White Tiger*, the writer has tried to record a kind of continuous murmur and growl beneath middle class life in India. He has tried to weave a really existing world, striking a chord of reality with readers in his novel. Besides, getting an account of Balram's transformation from a driver to a big entrepreneur, the reader also gets an opportunity to see India—a big country, its people, places, customs, traditions and systems.

In epistolary form, the narrator delivers his narrative with an artful technique—blending narration and description, reflection and revelation. Sometimes, the narrative also tends towards flashbacks and reminiscence, for while describing one event, the narrator is reminded of several other related events of his life which he wants to share with his readers. Ironic and satiric tone also forms the part of narration and binds the readers' interest throughout the novel. The narrative in the present novel encompasses largely commentary from the perspective of 'a half-baked' Indian. As a self-conscious narrator, he is always aware of himself as writer and gives commentary on the physical events and details in many different forms. Also there is no sentence or phrase to destroy the illusion that these are Balram's own words. The whole narration is in the form of a diary in which the narrator makes explicit reference to the fact that he is writing and telling his story. Moreover, autobiographical content forms a significant part of his narration. As he himself says, "The Autobiography of a Half-Baked Indian. That's what I ought to call my life's story" (10). The presence of Mr. Jiabao, the addressee, has been constantly felt thereby imparting the narration a realistic touch with use of such words as 'You see,' 'sir,' 'Your Excellency,' 'Mr. Jiabao,' 'Bear with me Mr. Jiabao' (9); 'Let me assure you' (10), 'Mr. Premier (11), 'Please understand, Your Excellency' (14).

The novel opens with an address to Mr. Wen Jiabao of Beijing from the desk of 'The White Tiger'—an entrepreneur—who claims to present 'the truth about Bangalore' and Indian entrepreneurs in response to the news that the Chinese Premier is scheduled to arrive the following week and wants to learn the truth about Bangalore which he is willing to divulge to him. The firm, straight and confident tone of the speaker in the opening pages prepares the readers for the truth they'll be getting in the story. Addressing the Chinese Premier, the narrator says, "I offer to tell you, free of charge, the truth about Bangalore. By telling you my life story" (6).

Along with flashbacks and past memories, the narration may be termed as episodic in the first half of the novel. While introducing himself through a poster and giving basic facts about his origin, height, weight, parentage and school, he also gives a picture of related systems by adding his own comments on various situations. While referring to his name 'Balram Halwai' alias

Munna, the narrator takes the readers back to his first day in school and narrates the incident when the teacher named him Balram for Munna meant just a boy.

> 'Didn't your mother name you?'
>
> 'She's very ill sir. She lies in bed and spews blood. She has got no time to name me.'
>
> 'And your father?'
>
> 'He's a rickshaw-puller, sir. He has got no time to name me.'
>
> 'Don't you have a granny? Aunts? Uncles?'
>
> 'They've got no time either.' (12)

The dialogue is then followed by his remarks: "now what kind of place is it where people forget to name their children?" (14). This very pattern is followed by the narrator many times in the novel. The above dialogue portrays Balram's childhood innocence marred by poverty and neglect. In another incident, while telling about his school, the speaker is reminded of his teacher—a big paan-and-spit man,' class rooms without duster or chairs, boys without uniforms, playing in classes, imitating his spitting style at the dirty walls while the teacher went to sleep which he usually did by noon.

He also narrates an incident of sudden inspection at his school when he was praised by the school inspector in front of his teacher by being called 'a white tiger' the rarest of the animal: "That's what you are, in this jungle" (34). Thus, through various experiences that he himself has experienced, the narrator, by simple episodes, shows as well as narrates his story to the reader, and at the same time in a realistic manner, reveals many more things related to Indian system of which he himself is a part which the reader tends to believe: "The reader responds to this type of narration with greater credulousness; he feels that the narrative is a true one because he has himself experienced the incidents and situations. In other words, by using the first person narrator, the novelist is able to create more convincingly the illusion of reality" (Dahiya 136-37).

Another feature of Balram's narration is his confessional mode. During his narration, he plainly confesses his flaws—dishonesty, insincerity, greed, hypocrisy, artificiality, cleverness, flattery, deceitfulness—and in this way, reveals his innermost feelings to the readers. By doing so, he wins the reader's faith and confidence. Many examples can be cited from the novel. As he tells, "I did my job with near total dishonesty, lack of dedication and insincerity. Instead of wiping out spots from tables and crushing coals, I used my time at the teashop in Laxmangarh to spy on every customer at every table and overhear everything they said" (52). And then he says, "No one else in Laxmangarh would hire me after that" (52).

When he comes to Dhanbad and starts looking for the job of a driver, walking from house to house, and comes to Stork's house, he at once starts his performance: "Swoosh!—As soon as the gate was open, I dived straight at the Stork's feet. No Olympic runner could have gone in as fast as I did through those gates. You should have seen me—what a performance of wails and kisses and tears! You'd think I'd been born into a caste of performing actors! And all the time, while clutching the Stork's feet, I was staring at his huge, dirty uncut toe-nails and thinking, what is he doing in Dhanbad? Why isn't he back home" (61). Here, comically, he reveals the dual aspect of his personality and shows the difference between his doing and saying. This account of his innermost feelings helps in making his narration convincing and realistic. At another time, he tells, "Over next two weeks I did things I am still ashamed to admit. I siphoned his petrol; I took his car to a corrupt mechanic who billed him for work that was not necessary; and three times, while driving back to Buckingham B, I picked up a paying customer" (230). Such self-conscious remarks by the narrator bring the reader back to his suspension of disbelief and his doubts about the narrator's reliability are dispelled.

One of the most potent devices that the narrator uses is satire. Satire operates in his description of various Indian systems and settings. Be it places or people, scenes or situations, events or characters, traditions or beliefs, the tone of the narrator is sharp, direct and bitter. As he puts it: "One fact about India is that you can take almost anything you hear about the country from the Prime Minister and turn it upside down and then you will have the truth about the thing" (15). While telling about the mockery of the government program of mid-day food at his school, in which each boy was to be given three rotis, yellow daal and pickle at lunch time, he says, "But we never ever saw rotis or yellow daal, or pickles and everyone knew why: the schoolteacher had stolen our lunch money" (33).

On police, he says, "I'm revealing the secret of a successful escape. The police searched for me in darkness: but I hid myself in light. In Bangalore!" (118). He further tells, "You'll see my friends when you visit Bangalore—fat, paunchy men swinging their canes, on Bridge Road, poking and harassing vendors and shaking them down for money. I'm talking of the police, of course" (299-300). Thus, he openly discusses several aspects of India 'shining' that we rather feel ashamed of. While exposing the wily and tainted politicians, he comments, "three of the ministers are currently in jail, but continue to be ministers" (98).

Thus, satire runs all through the narrative and constitutes the most powerful ingredient of the narrator's prose style. Sometimes, sarcastic comments are coupled with a touch of humour, for example, he says, "It's true that all these gods seem to do awfully little work—much like our politicians—and yet keep winning re-election to their golden thrones in heaven, year after year" (8). He has used satire as the main weapon to ridicule the prevailing corrupt practices, disparity, inequality and misuse of authority. Besides satire, irony also forms a substantial part of Balram's narration. It is ironic how he is forced out of school to work at a tea shop for breaking and smashing coals to repay the loan taken for a lavish dowry for his cousin although his name was recommended for a scholarship by the school inspector who also lauded him by calling him 'the white tiger.'

> A little later two boys come around from school to watch me. Then two more boys came; then two more. I heard giggling.
>
> 'What is the creature that comes along only once in a generation?' One boy asked loudly.
>
> 'The coal breaker,' another replied.
>
> And all of them began to laugh. (37)

Irony operates in his description of characters also. He tells how one day, when after giving bribe to ministers, Ashok and Mukesh were returning and the car is trapped in a jam and as he gives one rupee to a handicapped beggar who was moaning and groaning, Mukesh snubs him saying, "Who the hell told you to do that? Why the hell did you give that beggar a rupee" (241). Thus, ironically, he shows the meanness and insensitiveness of 'Mukesh sir.'

Thus, despite intruding into the narrative repeatedly through comments, Balram is successful in depicting the life of the poor and the class-related resentment in a convincing way. The reader is likely to find himself identifying with him in a variety of ways. Therefore, the reader feels himself involved in his affair and is not so much critical of the murder that he commits. It is through the narrator's point of view that the reader's opinion is formed. What is remarkable about the style of the narrator is his natural flow. In the simple style of the narrator, the reader, instead of remaining away from the events, becomes involved in it. With so much overlapping and interweaving of details, his narration is a series of engaging incidents and episodes. Since he has spent his life in India, he is not only a first-hand witness to intimate affairs but also an involved participant in the Indian milieu. It is not only in the way in which he tells his story, but in the details he remembers that Balram is true to himself. His narrative is unique in its ability to capture every minute detail and its emphatic breathless quality. His vivid presentation takes the readers very close to where the action is. To sum up, Aravind Adiga offers the truthful look at class struggle in modern India as seen through the eyes of the chauffeur Balram Halwai and in the latter's language.

Works Cited

Adiga, Aravind. *The White Tiger*. New Delhi: Harper Collins, 2009.

Dahiya, Bhim S. *Hemingway's The Sun Also Rises: A Critical Introduction*. New Delhi: Lakeside, 1986.

Vikas Swarup's *Q & A* : Focus on Style

SUSHEELA RANA

Before going into the intricacies of the various stylistic devices used in the above mentioned work, one must bear in mind that style is not something superimposed like a garnish on a blend, but the peculiar flavour and essence of a work of art emanating from a unique and individual blending of the ingredients. Further, all form is dictated by its content which is further directed by its *raison de etré*. Hence, style cannot be studied in exclusion of its content and circumstances of its genesis. It is no longer a petty endeavour by the natives to carve a sympathetic niche for themselves in the minds of the sahibs but introspective narratives by cosmopolitan citizens savouring a taste of India despite it being tangy and bitter. The didactic purpose of the contemporary intelligentsia is of course an honest appraisal of the gory details of the Indian subcontinent aimed at its metamorphosis. All such writing is from conscientious citizens wanting to see their country at a rightful and prestigious place on the global map. It does not matter whether the genre chosen is fiction as in the case of the present work or a critique like Nandan Nilekani's *Imagining India: Ideas for the New Century* or Narayanamurthy's *A Better India a Better World.*

Vikas Swarup, the creator of the novel *Q & A,* is a senior IFS officer, no novice, unaware of the fact that every syllable—its tone and tenor is pregnant with meanings –denotations, connotations and nuances. After all, what else is diplomacy if not a careful play on rhetoric! The narrative opens with a prologue which, in fact, is an epilogue as the virtual dossier on contemporary Indian scenario which he revisits. Every one of the loosely-strung incidents exposes a particular blot on the Indian social canvas.

The early allusions to Mahatma Gandhi, the contemporary Indian demi-god, and the myth of Lord Ram, who was banished to the jungle for fourteen years, as archetypes are not lost to the reader. Inspector Godbole (read Godse) is once again ready to assassinate Gandhi with the gory torture he metes out to the protagonist. The modern day Ram is banished to the slum jungle and will not be redeemed even after fourteen years. British hegemony is still thriving on the sub-continent and the various rungs of powers-that-be—the police inspector, the commissioner, the minister, the MNC channel bosses are the new links in the empire. The perspective is totally inverted in the film version where he treats it as the proverbial white man's burden to redeem this hell-hole called India.

In the novel, there is an element of hope hovering right from the beginning of the novel. In the prologue itself, Smita Shah, a lawyer, emerges to rescue Ram with the aid of the law of the land, thus reaffirming faith in it. It is noteworthy that the instrument of redemption chosen by the author is no *deux machina* Hanuman but an educated middle class young woman. There are few things very near the heart of Indians –films, religion, family, cricket, education and tradition. Swarup examines each one in great depth and with precision. The whole novel is an expose.

The novel opens like a Bollywood movie at the dramatic climax and goes into the genesis of the answers, using the flashback technique. The very first anecdote ensuing from the first question of the show *Kaun Banega Crorepati* that Ram plays is about the hero worship these screen gods enjoy. The masses are very disillusioned if they discover them to be capricious and immoral like ordinary mortals. The film version neatly glosses over the sexual perversions of the filmdom and takes special pleasure in highlighting the vital gutter Dharavi, the locale of the novel in Bollywood style. At times, these people fail to distinguish between real and reel life like the tragedy queen of eleventh question. She lives in a virtual glasshouse admiring her own reflections. She admits, 'We people who work in films become very vain. We get so used to seeing ourselves in make-up that we no longer have the courage to look in the mirror and see our real faces' (253) and later she commits suicide. Life always has some loose strings but the novel neatly ends with a suitable denouement: The Big B inspires the picaresque hero to keep a lucky coin like the character Jai of *Sholay*. What unites the loosely-strung episodes is the thread of a love story to add the filmi masala; the lovely maiden is in peril whom the hero rescues. The author leaves the reader in no doubt when he draws parallels throughout the narrative.

At the beginning of the novel, when Smita Shah, his lawyer, asks him to tell the truth, he says, "You mean like they say in the movies the truth, the whole truth and nothing but the truth" (30). Further,

> In films, they show a villain falling from the roof of a skyscraper and it seems as if he is floating in the air. He twists his legs and flaps his arms and screams AAAAAAAAAA. In real life, it does not happen like that at all. (85).
>
> In the films, they show you killing a man is as easy as popping a balloon. Bam, bam, bam . . . people in films fire guns as though bullets are going out of circulation. They kill people as we squash ants. Even a novice hero, who has never ever seen a gun in his life, is able to shoot and kill ten buddies in the villain's den from five hundred feet away. But real life is very different. It is easy to pick up a loaded gun and point it in someone's face. But when you know a real bullet will strike a real heart and the scarlet liquid will be blood and not tomato ketchup, you are forced to think twice. It is not easy to kill a man. You need to first switch off your brain. Drinking can do that. And so can anger. (351)

Swarup's narrative is full of sly digs on Indian complacency about religion, family, charity and ethics. In an *expose* style, all these are closely examined and found wanting. About the oft-claimed Indian stoicism, he makes Salim comment: "We Indians have this sublime ability to see the pain and misery around us and yet remain unaffected by it. So like a proper Mumbaiker, close your eyes, close your ears, close your mouth and you will be happy like me. Now go, it is time for my sleep" (84).

The author presents the picture of a dismal Indian education system when he remarks that, Putul a schoolboy has been given an assignment to write an essay on MY COW and Putul doesn't have a cow. (208) He is disillusioned by Indian research and sympathizes with Shantaram, talented astronomer edged out of the system by wily colleagues who enjoy the fruits of his labour. Other things close to the Indian hearts are defence services and cricket. The author finds them equally phoney. He candidly admits that the great Indian heritage is as grey as the Taj and as much of a fiction as Raju the guide's concoctions.

The novelist weaves twelve experiences or Bollywood-type stories into one novel with efficient artistry. Swarup introduces the reader to new and interesting characters and situations that flow smoothly from chapter to chapter despite the bouncing around in time and place. The protagonist's name reminds one of Bollywood movies like *Amar Akbar Antony* and themes of friendship between characters belonging to different religions in various movies. His experience as a tourist guide is reminiscent of an older blockbuster movie. *The Guide* based on a novel by the famous Indian novelist R.K. Narayan. Salim's hero worship of Arman Ali reveals the ever-present popularity of Bollywood movies which this novel resembles. The fast pace of the novel leaves the reader breathless and enchanted. Robin Osborne rightly comments about the novel: "Insightful about India and frequently hilarious, this is a remarkable debut novel."

Works Cited

Nilekani, Nandan. *Imagining India—Ideas for the New Century.* Penguin Allen Lane, 2008

Narayana Murthy. R. *A Better India, A Better World.* London: Penguin, 2009.

Osborne, Robin. Book Review—Q & A <http://www.suite101.com/content/book-review-q-a-by-vikas-swarup>

Vikas Swarup *Q & A*. New Delhi: Black Swan, 2005.

Chutnifying the Text: A View on the Split Synchrony and Literary Globalisation

ALESSANDRO MONTI

> *Chatni*: Sauce, indigenous sauce; a kind of acid sauce or marmalade. (Hindi Dictionary)
> *Chatni Banana*: To transform into pulp, to beat up thoroughly. (Hindi Dictionary)
> *Chatni:* Chutneys can be made from different ingredients but popular chutneys include mango chutney, tamarind chutney and coriander. Coconut chutney is generally served with south Indian food. (Hindi and Urdu Phrasebook)
> *Chutney*: A type of pickle, originally from India, made with fruit, vinegar, spices, sugar. (British Dictionary)
> *Chutney*: A sweet and spicy relish made from fruit, spices, sugar and vinegar. (American World English Dictionary)

Chutney is a word across, a sort of now settled semantic migrant that has been scattered into the interstices of another's language. It indicates retroactively a colonial encounter and a deliberate mixture concerning difference, either in taste or in flavour. It constitutes an extended metaphor of contact and change, of colonial expansion and of cultural backdrop. A concise text in itself, chutney stretches the national allegory of affiliated identity up to the continuous slippage of values introduced by high hybridisation. Its procedures of transcolonial assimilation into the Western (or British, at least) dietary system reveal gluttony and simultaneously restore to visibility the archaic and voracious gastric figure that disrupts the linear genealogies that indicate development and span different acts of enunciation. My transoceanic metaphor concerning food represents a contested territory of postcolonial writing, beyond and notwithstanding the dubious or vicarious pleasures of change and assimilation. This step provides a loaded battleground for performative repetitions of meaning and organised affective diet. In a nutshell, my metaphor is caught, rather than being illustrated by it, in the diglossic transition from the phonetically hostile *chatni* to the more familiar and palatable term chutney.

Such an act of lexical migrancy releases parodic strategies of narrational rhetoric, whose catachrestic nature illustrates displacement and deformation. The emergence of a literary language grounded on disjunctive sequences of lexical diaspora lays bare what is untranslatable in this aesthetic of exchange. The gap goes beyond the mere severance of continuity and *does* transcend the blessed proliferation of cross-cultural texts. We should be able to identify an element of resistance in such operations that re-inscribe identities or meanings. The lexeme chutney is obscured by a borderline feeling of anxiety and retroactive belonging, one that dramatises hybridity as an unfinished zone of regret and self-effacement. This hybrid discourse of disavowal appears in the non-dialogic script of the Anglo-Indian voice. We should mention the now forgotten *Chutney Lyrics*, sketches of mild-flavoured colonial apories of differentiated presence that half-work the notion of linguistic and cultural chutnification, through a dispossessing feeling of migrancy from the native West to the East.[1]

Thus, the term *chutney* suggests a double passage of sour assimilation in the fragmented system of signs, one that produces heterogeneous forms of diasporic human identities and simultaneously rehearses suburban fantasies of tamed exoticism: from composite *masala* to cockney pickle, I would say. This early instance of colonial globalisation raises however the issue of difference, seen as the agency that defers the inscribed meaning to a retroactive fantasy of modified genealogical belonging. Bhabha argues the debate in terms of gathering: a chiasmatic rescue of the past and the refusal of whatever apologetic nostalgia.[2] As such, chutnification transfers a scattered meaning across the middle passage of metaphor, so as to start a distanced view through an impression of imagined contiguity. This colonial incorporation of the archaic gathers authority by means of a decisive slippage of ingredients and selective procedures: assimilation represents a disseminative strategy of previous struggle and final globalised counter-liminality.

The harsh conflict with the archaic of which Bhabha speaks is signified by Rushdie in *Midnight's Children*, when in the first pages of his novel, he illustrates his selective procedures of discursive strategy by introducing a mixed, or chutnified, metaphor of similarity between the narrative text, food (or the dietary norms concerning it) and the human body,

> Family history, of course, has its proper dietary laws. One is supposed to swallow and digest only the permitted parts of it, the *halal* portions of the past, drained of their redness, their blood. Unfortunately, this makes the stories less juicy; so I am about to become the first and only member of the family to flout the laws of *halal*. Letting no blood escape from the body of the tale, I arrive at the unspeakable part; and, undaunted, press on.[3]

The term *halal* (one that is fraught with stiff overtones of self-righteous purity and assertions of un-negotiable discrimination) foregrounds a kind of critically loaded globalisation, one that excludes any possibility of free movement across the interstices of communal belonging and only recognises affiliated identities. Rushdie cuts across such exclusive areas of darkness and by doing so, he disrupts the archives nourished by sectarian belonging and sequences of uninterrupted cultural lineage. His textual policy of chutnification surmounts discrimination and inscribes *de facto* his script into the sphere of the forbidden (*haraam*). Whereas colonial hybridisation assimilates and modifies according to taste, the category of *halal* globalises by means of taboos and exclusions. Instead of proposing a unified point of view it introduces division, so as to pull the discourse away from the present, and consequently takes archaic modes of homogenisation. Rusdhie replaces heterogeneity for this kind of homogeneity. His gargantuan rediscovery of the body and its equalisation with a full-blooded text ("letting no blood escape from the body of the tale") restores analogical constructs that are grounded on globalising images of food.

To find a similar vision of reactive resistance, we have to move back to the body of Bharat Devi in *Anandmath* (1982) by Bankimchandra, in which we view the stages of anticolonial resistance through the different aspects assumed by the goddess. These two instances authorise the religious or national archive through select representations of the body seen as a reconstituted unique: a cultural continuum whose morphological features correspond to the decent and anti-grotesque body of which Bakhtin speaks: a closed whole, with no blemishes or fissures, a stopped hole that allows neither passage nor reproduction.[4] This body is interpreted by Rushdie in specific terms of grotesque representation ("the past has drifted into me [. . .] history pours out of my fissured body" [37]). Of course, the paradigmatic sequence into-out evokes the grotesque and unique image of the eaten-eating world that Bakhtin finds in Rabelais.[5] In particular, the very act of death ("pours out of my fissured body," in Rushdie) coincides with the act of birth, such as analysed by Bakhtin apropos of the episode that narrates how Gargantua came to the world. This reorganisation of the body seen as a sign (or rather, as a system of signs) introduces us to the notion of the leaking archive, that is the response that Rushdie gives to the imagined un-fissured body of the anti-grotesque tradition. Here two different and antinomic models of globalisation (respectively the archaic and the grotesque) are at hand. The former postulates indivisibility and claims globalisation to itself, as an exclusive pattern that allows only *halal* rules, whereas the latter acts within an interstitial space, within an in-between zone of contact, whose archaeological roots must be found in the bicorporeal image outlined by Bakhtin and whose slightly chaotic growth occurs in Bhabha. We should refer, for instance, to his imagined version of the migrant, one who lives (or thrives or survives, following circumstances) in a borderline condition between metaphorical states of death and rebirth, loss "pouring out" and change or even gain.

To me, the discursive strategies of postcolonial discourse adopted by Bhabha endorse the demarginalised figure of the migrant in terms of excess and too oblique presence. However, I would not argue at all, in the wake of Gayatri Spivak and Bhabha himself, about a catachrestic agency that opens up an interruptive time-lag in the progressive myth of modernity.[6] I would rather speak of the exorbitance introduced by the migrant in the Western scenario. The notion of exorbitance deploys possibilities of grotesque representation, that is, it recognises the functional role assumed by the separate and autonomous parts into the definition of individuality. Then, the fact of splitting apart constitutes a metaphor of fullness, a multiplicity (or a multiplication) of the cracks (or in more mundane language, of the body fissures) that explode in *Midnight's Children*,

> Please believe that I am falling apart.
>
> I am not speaking metaphorically, nor is this the opening gambit of some melodramatic, riddling, grubby appeal for pity. I mean quite simply that I have begun to crack all over like an old jug—that my poor body, singular, unlovely, buffeted by too much history, subjected to drainage above and drainage below, mutilated by doors, brained by spittoons, has started coming apart at the seams. In short, I am literally disintegrating, slowly for the moment, although there are signs of acceleration. I ask you only to accept (as I have accepted) that I shall eventually crumble in (approximately) six hundred and thirty million particles of anonymous, and necessarily oblivious dust. This is why I have resolved to confide in paper, before I forget (We are a nation of forgetters). (36)

The Rabelaisian quality of this mock extended catalogue transposes the culturally bloated identity of the migrant, such as seen by Bhabha, from the underworld of dissonance and miscellaneous gathering, one that turns ascription into hybridity, to the imagined dual intersecting body figured by Bakhtin. In particular, Rushdie locates the body of Saleem in a zone of encounter between the collapse of death and the revival of memory. In Rabelais, the act of ravenous gluttony that precedes the birth of Gargantua integrates the heavy physiological surface of the episode with a simultaneously generative movement. Likewise, the battered and splintered body of Saleem substitutes an implied metaphor of continuity (represented by the possibilities of keeping a total memory of the past) for the forbidding notion of the archive. A further element of correlation with the analysis developed by Bakhtin is given by the analogy between the falling apart of the imagined body of the narrator and the falling apart of the social body. Of course, this unbalancing split could be viewed as a parody of some myths of origin, such as the ones embodied by the Hindu story of Purusa. However, the processes of splitting and successive chutnification in *Midnight's Children* suggest a genealogical deconstruction of identity, rather than foregrounding stereotyped images of social order and unruffled accommodation of integrated cultures.

According to Bhabha, the subaltern or metonymic are neither empty nor full, neither part nor wholly. This exercise of authority is then grounded on conflict and evokes a kind of supplementary disavowal in the enunciation of national identity. The double inscription of which Bhabha speaks operates on lines that are analogous to the metamorphoses implied by the globalising act of chutnification, whose teleology of partial homogeneity is surmounted by the adaptive reconstruction of the archaic. (In my instance, the native *chatni*, tamed into the more palatable *chutney*). I would like to extrapolate two more hints from the discourse of belonging (or re-possession), one that I would reproduce by assimilating the terms of translated enunciation and transferential subversion articulated by Bhabha, namely, the metonymical quality that we should be able to recognise in the globalising text of the migrant writer and the acknowledgement of growth (expressed by the emergence of the organic) as an inter-cutting (or hybrid) process. Consequently, we should focus our attention on the close connection between the foetus of the future narrator in his mother's womb and the correlative expansion of the intensified discourse into a text, a book, even an encyclopaedia,

> By the time the rains came at the end of June, the foetus was fully formed inside her womb. Knees and nose were present; and as many heads as would grow were already in position. What had been (at the beginning) no bigger than a full stop had expanded into a comma, a word, a sentence, a paragraph, a chapter; now it was bursting into more complex developments, becoming, one might say, a book—perhaps an encyclopaedia—even a whole language. (111)

The organic metaphor that equates the human body and its growth to the book and its normative power (the encyclopaedia) is structurally rendered into the apparently low language of food, an idiom that Bakhtin hyphenates in the composed definition material-physical (that is, pertaining to the body). This transgressive strategy instructs analogies of discursive synecdoche, so as to posit a borderline identity of the migrant, one that defuses the sliding inscription of his belonging into the liminality of the assimilated stranger and finally re-inscribes a transnational expression of the globalised (or open) archive. Thus, the correlated motifs of birth and growth (whose starting points are constituted by the formation of the foetus) involve both the human body and the postcolonial text. They may be developed so as to shape a superorganic image of reproduction beyond decay and waste. To preserve (in other words, to chutnify) becomes a further key metaphor of organic (and textual as well) imagery, one that finally encapsulates disseminative sequences of identity, which remind me of the principle of super-individual life (or multi-semantic body, to me) argued by Bakhtin.[7]

Rushdie abolishes whatever difference between the truth of the narrator and the rhetoric construction of the text, between the period of pregnancy, the low act of delivery and the generative act of writing. However, we cannot just interpret this movement towards homogeneity in terms of situational consciousness, the national allegory of which Fredric Jameson speaks, perhaps a too comprehensive notion that sublimates how "the telling of the individual story and the individual experience cannot but ultimately involve the whole laborious telling of the community itself."[8] We should disconnect this analogical discourse of national memory that has been retold and of private affiliation that has been made general. Such loaded moments of cohesion are questioned *in toto* by Rushdie, who begins *Midnight's Children* by articulating disjunctive sequences of synchronic ambivalence, between the crumbling body of the narrator and the growth in progress of the fictional text. This imagined condition of emptiness and simultaneously of coming fullness (or re-birth) might be referred to estranging strategies of calculated synecdoche, one in which the holistic unity of the narrative is indicated by the impending dispersal or fragmentation of the body. Of course, this procedure reminds us of the well-known low feasting that in Rabelais anticipates the birth of Gargantua, to the effect that the physiological dissolution of the maternal bowels coincides with the coming out of the hero. This state of falling apart requires counter-images of preservation against the flowing away of the vital fluids that give life to the body (the cracks and fissures of the bloated and bursting of Saleem).

The multisemantic process of fragmentation, involving as it does procedures both of filling and emptying, is forelighted by Rushdie at the beginning of the novel, "while I sit like an empty pickle jar in the pool of Anglo-poised light" (14). We should be able to detect in the whole passage a strategy of narration that regulates the continuous slippage from family story to categories of national affiliation (or dis-affiliation), from the apparently smooth surface of mnestic communality to the cleavage introduced by the "Anglo-poised light." Chutnification stands here as a sign of compromised nationality: it preserves the otherwise interrupted flow of memory but displays simultaneously a bitter sense of displacement. It makes also possible intersections of meaning, ones whose hybridised nature is well exemplified by the difference in taste and spelling between the *deshi* food and the English-transferred chutney. Thus the term lays bare globalisation with a difference: as a literary marker of style and language it deploys a Janus-like quality, one of dissonance and agonistic co-presence rather than of interfaced continuity of values. To misquote Bhabha, Rushdie adopts chutnification to express temporality rather than historicity. He has no apologies to show.[9]

The case is different with another chutnified (rather than chutnifying) text, *The God of Small Things* (1997) by Arundathi Roy. In this novel the metaphor of preservation dramatises the narrative of individual experiences as the rhetorical device that illustrates history. The huge vats in which fruit and vegetables are boiled and reduced to formless pulp represent a sweetened version of the national archive. The ultimate and too clever symbol of this synthesis is well represented by the finally hot encounter between the subaltern and the lady. Arundathi Roy replaces the easy pathos of the love story for the splintering image of the grotesque body. She restores tears and copulation, whereas Rushdie had introduced laugh and sexual impotence. The effective move from Salman Rushdie to Arundathi Roy strikes a note of bourgeois feasting and reductive manipulation of the organic metaphor of textual growth. She churns words into sophisticated and useless puns, whose transgressive range had already been questioned, and shrugged away, by a wiser Bharati Mukherjee in her novel *The Tiger's Daughter*,

> That first winter in Poughkeepsie she had been given Sartre and Camus, Rilke and Mann, and the Joyce beyond *Dubliners*, and her closed little heart had been flooded. She had even begun writing stories about Calcutta based on the style and subtleties of Joyce and she had stopped only when they had become too easy, too obvious.[10]

Whereas Bharati Mukherjee adopts a stance of disaffiliation from the memories of the *archaic* margin that she has left at home, Arundathi Roy saturates the same interstitial space of vacancy. Both writers refuse the regret expressed by the chutnification of the literary text and separate the act of resistance from a condition of existential *maroonage*. Instead of bursting away as Rushdie does, they re-imagine the details of loss and nostalgia in the lives of the migrants, so as to avoid underdevelopment and defeat: both of them scatter apologies and disseminate fantasies that foreground the select disavowal of their origin.

They interpret the language of modernity in personalised terms of displacing intersections between their own (imagined) biographies and the national symbols of locality. Their critical gaze moves through subjectivity as the unique form of "lived historical memory," well against the disruptive exercise of narrative authority embodied by Salman Rushdie. If we want to detect crucial forms of ubiquitous presence, and analyse unquestionable movements of doubleness in writing, we should consider again the initial generative metaphor of birth in *Midnight's Children*. The analogical foetus of the future narrator grows before our astonished eyes, a powerful object of discursive signification that turns the petty chronicle of family life into an iterated sign of decentred belonging: from physiological accumulation to the recursive pedagogy of the performed text.

However, this passage deploys a further projection of affective memories that negotiate identity by means of a contested transition of territories. The ambiguous hint to the many heads possessed by the foetus ("and as many heads would grow were already in position") constitutes an image that should remind us of the multiple limbs that sprout from the bodies of the Hindu gods and goddesses. Such a collapse of the rules of finitude that we usually associate with the rational configuration of the human body indicates cultural and ironic miscegenation. It *does* invert the rigidity of the *halal* imposition in favour of the plastic re-thinking of the full body. This process of regained exorbitance from the rules that circumscribe identity and claim select belonging may be viewed as a modern adaptation of the grotesque globalisation of the human body made by Rabelais. It also shifts the agencies of signification from the dietary rules of *halal* to the plastic sites figured by the culture and the myths of the Hindus. This ability in transferring or translating the grounds of knowledge, beyond the punishing practice of negation, posits the issue of literary globalisation in terms of supplementary iteration of meanings: the virtually many-headed Saleem.

Once again Rushdie, the magic tightrope walker, moves across the boundaries and the closures of the postcolonial writer. He eludes the vexed question of the origin, such as represented by the stereotyped aura of revenge that the Western and the Westernising script usually associate with the proliferating reproduction of the "archaic" traits in the culture of the East. To illustrate my point, and testify how Rushdie goes beyond the estranging movement that confirms the binary vision of the authoritative migrant, it is worth considering the cases of *Jasmine* and *Wife*. In both of them Bharati Mukherjee metamorphoses her persecuted heroines into the savage persona of Kali, so as to make possible and underline the metonymic intervention of difference in the deferred maintenance of a performative and exhibited identity. In particular, the writer accommodates the anxiety of her counter-response and produces an imagined construct of racial fantasy, expressed by the gothic figure of the American would-be rapist Half-Face (a character drawn directly from the pages of *Dick Tracy*).

Bharati Mukherjee masquerades the grotesque vision of the represented body in the discursive images of alien presence and menace, so as to shift our gaze from the East to the West. Her reaction is however grounded on a sign of atavistic memory and regressive power of competitive reaction,

> It was the murkiness of the mirror and a sudden sense of mission that stopped me. What if my mission was not yet over? I didn't *feel* the passionate embrace of Lord Yama that could turn a kerosene flame into a lover's caress. I could not let my personal dishonour disrupt my mission. There would be plenty of time to die; I had not yet burned my husband's suit. I had not stood under the palm tree of the college campus.
>
> I extended my tongue, and sliced it. Hot blood dripped immediately in the sink. . . . I wanted that moment when he saw me above him as he had last seen me, naked, but now with my mouth open, pouring blood, my red tongue out.[11]

A similar tactic is rehearsed in the slightly controversial *Wife*, in which the killing of the husband reminds us of the ritual sacrifice of a goat to the goddess Kali,

> She sneaked up on him and chose a spot, her favourite spot just under the hairline, where the mole was getting larger and browner, and she drew an imaginary line of kisses because she did not want him to think she was the impulsive, foolish sort who acted like a maniac just because the husband was suffering from insomnia. She touched the mole very lightly and let her fingers draw a circle around the delectable spot, then she brought her right hand up and with the knife stabbed the magical circle once, twice, seven times, each time a little harder, until the milk in the bowl of cereal was a pretty pink and the flakes were mushy and would have embarrassed any advertiser, and then she saw the head fall off.[12]

The fetished reaction and reactive appearance of Kali, to redeem an undervalued feminine identity, represents a fulfilled and retroactive imposition of difference. The return of the darkened Devi is poised against a hegemonic sign of gendered authority, one that imposes rape or subtle discrimination. Kali embodies here a movement against ambivalence and separation, so as to lend authority to the individualised conflicts that restore comforting rules of rigid self-identification and prejudicial authority. Bharati Mukherjee recuperates, through strategies of "archaic" resistance, a de-hybridised source of power and primal identification.

With Arundhati Roy, the eastern body (whose representative identity is conveyed to us by the copulating pair at the end of the book, the union of Shiva with Kali, as an over-enthusiast Western commentator wrote), can be only viewed through an act of vulgar voyeurism. Bharati Mukherjee returns overtly to the folk Hindu type, given that her avenging women are seen as icons of Kali, the female destroyer. We miss in both situations the grotesque vision of estrangement and of passage across that we *do* find in Rushdie. By doing so, he curtails the agony of direct confrontation and exercises his intervening authority by an act of disavowal, so as to deconstruct the rules that control the representation of the postcolonial imagined world. Instead of evoking death through a metaphor of regret and astute painful memory (as Arundhati Roy does) or to attend his transitions to the mood of revenge set by Bharati Mukherjee, Rushdie opts for a kind of grotesque heteroglossia, whose range moves away from the rigidity of *halal* to the free plasticity of Hinduism and whose multiplicity of relations deploys a universal language of narration and counter-miscegenation. He devises a true chutney of style, simultaneously sweetish and sour, indigenous and cosmopolitan: a globalising script in which East and West meet at last.

NOTES

1. R.C. Caldwell, *The Chutney Lyrics, A Collection of Comic Pieces in Verse on Indian Subjects*, Madras, Higginbotham, 1871.
2. Homi Bhabha, *The Location of Culture*, London and New York, Routledge, 1994, p. 139.
3. Salman Rushdie, *Midnight's Children*, New York, Penguin, 2000 (1980), p. 62.
4. M.M. Bakhtin, *L'opera di Rabelais e la cultura popolare*, Torino, Einaudi, 1979 (1965), p. 350. English title, *Rabelais and Folk Culture of the Middle Ages and Renaissance.*
5. *Ibidem*, p. 242.
6. See also Bhabha, pp. 183-84: "Gayatri Spivak has usefully described the 'negotiation' of the postcolonial position 'in terms of reversing, displacing and seizing the apparatus of value-coding,' constituting a catachrestic space: words or concepts wrested from their proper meaning, 'a concept-metaphor without an adequate referent' that perverts its embedded context. Spivak continues, 'Claiming catachresis from a space that one cannot want to inhabit [the sentence, sententious] yet must criticize [from outside the sentence] is then, the deconstructive predicament of the postcolonial."
7. Bakhtin, p. 247.
8. Fredric Jameson, "Third World Literature in the Era of Multinational Capitalism," *Social Text* (Fall 1986), p. 69.
9. Bhabha, p. 140.
10. Bharati Mukherjee, *The Tiger's Daughter*, Markham, Ontario, Penguin, 1987 (1971), p. 45.
11. Bharati Mukherjee, *Jasmine*, New York, Grove Weidenfeld, 1989, pp. 117-18.
12. Bharati Mukherjee, *Wife*, Markham, Ontario, Penguin, 1990 (1975), pp. 212-13.

Narrative Strategies in Qurratulain Hyder's *River of Fire*

UMED SINGH

The common perception about Qurratulain Hyder's *River of Fire* (1998) is that it is a work of translation. But it is not a work of translation as Hyder calls the English version a transcreation of her Urdu novel *Aag ka Dariya* (1959). The transcreated work which emanates from the old one incorporates the author's fresh perceptions and ideas on various issues/ themes that she broached in her original Urdu creation. The novel offers a difficult reading for those who are unfamiliar with the cultural history of India as Hyder subverts the notion of 'grand narratives' and narrates the story in fragments. The novelist has used various narrative strategies to recreate and unfold two-and-a-half millennia of Indian history. There are recurrent names, recurrent themes and recurrent motifs which impart unity and cohesion to an apparently disjointed but complex narrative. Gautam, Champak, Hari Shankar, Kamaluddin, Cyril Ashley, Nirmala—all re-appear in different roles and guises and retain their names all through the narrative.

Hyder's preoccupation with the long period of Indian history i.e. from 4th century B.C to the partition and post-partition period makes this narrative rich and varied both in tone and tenor. The first fifty pages of the novel describe India in fourth century B.C; then there is a sudden jump in the narrative and the readers are transported to fifteenth century when the Mughal empire was gaining a foothold in India. The second half of the novel deals with the 'present time' i.e. the partition and post-partition phase of Indian history. Imbued with 'historical sense,' Hyder perceives not only the pastness of the past but also of its presence and, to invoke T.S. Eliot's concept of 'tradition,' she is conscious of her 'place' and 'time' in the 'whole existing order.' The beauty of her novel lies in the fact that it resists any easy categorization. One may read it as a historical novel, a partition novel and a novel depicting the clash of cultures. It deals with all major signifiers of the history of Indian subcontinent but it does not allow any single thread to dominate the others. If one does not go by the space allotted to various phases of Indian history, one finds that the novel neither privileges the early period of Indian history nor the Muslim era nor Hyder foregrounds the experience of colonialism as the most significant traumatic event of Indian history. The present paper seeks to explore the narrative strategies which sustain the long, complex but rich narrative of *River of Fire.*

No doubt, the narrative of *River of Fire* observes chronology but there are big 'gaps' and silences all through the novel. There are four plots/stories set in different epochs of history. The first plot is about Gautam and his intimate association with Hari Shankar, Champak, Nirmla, Sujata and others. The second plot is set in the Islamic period and revolves around Kamaluddin, the central character who is shown in intimate relationship with Bano, a Muslim girl, and Champavati, a Hindu girl. The third story in the colonial period unfolds the story of Cyril Ashley who maintains close relationship with Sujata Debi, Champa Jan and Marie Teresa. The postcolonial period tells the story of Champa Ahmad, Gautam Nilamber, Cyril Ashley, Kamaluddin, Nirmala etc. Apparently these stories are not linked together though some of the characters repeat in these four stories with or without slight twist in their names. But there is a subtle connection between these stories as names such as Gautam Nilamber, Champa, Sujata and Hari Shankar recur throughout the narrative which covers the period of two and a half millennium. The life and pursuits of the characters, their sense of failure and futility in different episodes seem alike.

Hyder weaves a rich texture in *River of Fire* where 'form' and 'content' enrich each other reciprocally. The novelist employs both 'mimetic' and 'diegetic,' to use Gerard Genette's vocabulary, modes of narration to capture the nuances of human life and existence. The mimetic mode of narration 'shows' or 'dramatises' the action. The action is "represented in a 'scenic' way, with a specified setting" and dialogues containing direct speech are used. The diegetic mode, on the other hand, conveys action "in a more 'rapid' or 'panoramic' or 'summarizing' way"[2] and no attempt is made to create an illusion that events are taking place before the eyes of the viewers. Hyder uses these two modes of narration alternately i.e. moving from 'mimetic' to 'diegetic,' and back again, for encompassing the rich and varied human experience. Note the following conversation between Champak and Gautam Nilamber.

> "May I have some rice and . . ."
>
> "You are just like our parrots. You repeat the same phrase day after day. Don't you know any other words?" *Champak asked him playfully.*
>
> "We are not supposed to indulge in unnecessary conversation with laity, especially females."
>
> "Are you training to be a Prohit?" *asked Nirmala.*
>
> "Yes, indeed."
>
> "Can you perform some rituals quickly to bring my brother, Prince Hari, back?"
>
> "Yes, I can. I will have to come here daily at a certain time, if you get me all the rare ingredients required for the havan."
>
> "I will," *she said eagerly.* He realised how easy it was to deceive women in these matters (26).

From the above extract, it is evident that Hyder is "showing" the action through the conversation between the two characters, princess Nirmala and Gautam Nilamber from the Forest University of Shravasti. The conversation takes place and the actual spoken words are given in inverted commas and the 'tagging' is given to indicate the name of the speaker. The underlined expressions indicate the name of the speaker. The sentence 'He realised how easy it was to deceive women in these matters.' comes from the 'authorial person,' i.e., a character who speaks the 'voice' of the author. Hyder makes frequent use of this narrative technique to get the tale told and enable the reader to read the mind of her characters.

The plot of *River of Fire* is episodic in nature and depicts selected historical periods of Indian history. There are sudden and quick jumps from one epoch to the other. There are frequent references to places and personages echoing the history from the period of antiquity to the postcolonial era. The names of Chanakya, Chandragupt Maurya and the glory of Patliputra and the wisdom of Lord Buddha and the very mention of the river Saryu instantly transport the readers back to the Classical Age. Note the following description:

> Then he jumped into the water and began swimming against the current.
>
> He had reached midstream. A forceful torrent came rushing and carried him close to the other shore. He struggled hard against the waves but the current was more powerful. . . . He was exhausted and panted heavily. He closed his eyes and clung to the rock. Time was pushing the torrent forward and there was a seemingly infinite expanse of water all around . . . a stone which has been in the past will remain in the future as well. But he couldn't hold on to the rock for more than a few seconds with his stumped fingers. The angry waves of the Saryu passed over Gautam.
>
> Syed Abul Mansar Kamaluddin arrived at the river bank at full gallop. The Saryu flowed majestically in front of him (53-54).

It is Gautam Nilamber who jumps into the Saryu but the man who emerges on the other side of the bank of the Saryu is not Gautam Nilamber but Syed Abul Mansar Kamaluddin of the Islamic period. Hyder very artistically squeezes the time and the reader is instantly transported from Classical Age to the fifteenth century.

The novel is unique in its structure and deals simultaneously with four historical epochs of Indian history. Champak, the daughter of the Chief Minister, is an important woman character in the first story. She is betrothed to Prince Hari who becomes a Buddhist *bhikshu* and shows little concern for Champak. She falls in love with Gautam but the war separates the lovers and she is finally captured and forced to join the harem of an old but influential person. With the passage of time, she loses her physical charm but she remains attached to Gautam. They meet by chance in the theatre at Patliputra.

> Champak sat in the front row, dressed in purple silk, loaded with gold ornaments. She was accompanied by a little boy and her maid. When she saw his crippled hands, burning tears welled up in her eyes. . . . The woman he had been searching for all these years—there she sat on the floor, cross-legged, with a child beside her. A prosperous housewife and mother. (47)

In the second story, Champak becomes Champavati, a Hindu girl. She is the sister of a learned Brahmin pandit in Ayodhya. She is ready to convert to Islam in order to marry Syed Abdul Mansur Kamaluddin. But Kamal, the wandering scholar, never returns, and eventually she joins a band of Vaishnav *sannyasins* and retires to the city of Brindaban. The pattern of the union and separation of lovers repeats and Hyder unfolds a story which enacts the drama of human suffering. Man easily reconciles with the situation and transfers his affection and passion to another woman but woman is always waiting for her lover, and is always suffering. The following description from the second story illustrates the truth.

> And let's admit, a fellow wants variety. I'm afraid I have almost forgotten princess Bano. These infidel women have a charm of their own. They are faithful, shy, docile. They worship their husbands as demi-gods and touch their feet in obeisance every morning. They put the man on a pedestal and sing songs in their praise. That is how it ought to be. . . . Here the roles are reversed –man is the beloved, the woman pines for him and is forever waiting for him. (76).

The theme of suffering and endless wait of a woman for her lover continues in the third story also. Here Champa Jan is a rich and influential courtesan who entertains the elite including British Nabab and Abdul Mansur Kamaluddin, Ali Reza Bahadur known as Nabab Kamman. She loses her heart to a Royal East India Company servant Gautam Nilambar Dutt who betrays her and she is endlessly waiting for him. Time moves and robs Champa of her charm and gradually she becomes a *chowdhrain* of *twaifs* in the princely state of Oudh or old Lucknow. The novelist describes the plight of Champa in the evening of her life:

> The beggar woman repeated the common form of blessing prevalent in Shia-oriented Lucknow: "May God give no other grief except the grief for Hussain. . . . One pice, only one pice."
>
> Gautam Nilambar froze. The late Nabab Kamman had told him about Champa Jan who had become a beggar at the railway station and waited for passengers from Calcutta. He shivered as it struck him that mendicant could be Champa. Was she? He adjusted his glasses and peered out. She stood on the roadside like a shadow. . . . A destitute, toothless woman had been waiting unreasonably at the railway station for an old man to come back. . . . He gave her a rupee. (177-78)

The fourth plot is set in the postcolonial period and tells the story of Champa, Gautam, Hari Shankar, Nirmala who happen to be friends in a college. The story also involves Kamal, Amir, Tehmina and several others from both Hindu and Muslim communities. Like a motif, Champa re-emerges in this story also. As usual, she is an incarnate of beauty who makes friends with various young men including Gautam Nilamber and Cyril Ashley in England. She does not marry either of the two and returns to India and eventually she opts for legal profession in Benares.

The fourth story covering almost half of the space of the book is very complex as far as its structure is concerned. The locale changes very frequently as it deals with the final years of the Raj. The characters, most of them are young men and women, go abroad for higher education. The scene shifts to Cambridge and London. Meanwhile the political situation in India worsens as a result of the formation of The Muslim League and its aftermath. Interestingly the novelist does not focus on the freedom struggle movement, an unforgettable event of Indian history of that time, but she observes keenly the impact of the event on the lives of the characters. For Hyder in the novel, the impact is more important than the event.

There is no doubt about the fact that 'time' is the central theme of the novel and time with its cyclic and circular movement imparts unity and continuity to an apparently disjointed narrative of the novel. It is illustrated by the fact that the stories in different epochs follow a uniform pattern. It also appears that this novel essentially has one story which happens four times albeit with minor changes. The novel tells a tale about men and women, their union and separation, their love and lust, and their ability/inability to adjust with the changing times. The quest for meaning in life and companionship takes these characters from one place to the other. The quest is always there. If one has attained the object of desire, he /she desires for something else. The moment of satiety, perhaps, never comes. It appears that human life is full of paradoxes and uncertainties. The trials and tribulations experienced by various characters in the novel illustrate this truth. Gautam desires the company of Champak; Hari, on the other hand, wants to get rid of Champak to whom he is betrothed.

The journey motif in the novel is very strong and there is hardly any episode which is without travellers who move from one place to the other. The travellers undertake journey due to some impulse or compulsions, maybe for pleasure, profit, poverty, displacement due to war, spiritual quest, education etc. The travellers move from one place to the other within India and outside India; freely associate with men and women who come into their contact and form relationships and then break human bonds. They make love, marry and beget children. If there is love and union, there is desertion and estrangement too. Human life is full of paradoxes. Time is an invisible enemy which thwarts the aspirations of men and women engaged in various pursuits. In *River of the Fire* 'Time' is a recurrent motif which imparts unity to the fragmentary narrative pattern of the novel. Harish Narang aptly remarks:

> A linearly progressing Time brings changes, and change can be a harbinger of grief or joy. Should one then take sides? That would be too easy, she confides to us, too simplistic, for these issues cannot be settled by referring to the material world alone. What counts for Q. Hyder are the human spirit and the relationships through which it blossoms forth. And that is where the linearity of Time

> turns into a spiral, bringing recognizable moments back to us if we have the necessary sensibility.[3]

Irony seems to be an organising principle of Hyder's narrative art. She skilfully builds irony into the texture of her novel. The novel seems to suggest that men and women are victim of time and history. The high and mighty, bold and beautiful—all are victim of time and history. Most of the characters in the novel feel the invisible and invincible forces of time and history which reduce bold and beautiful human beings into non-entities.

In the first story, Gautam Nilamber is fatally wounded by the invading army of Chandra Gupta. He becomes a wandering actor and then jumps into the river, never to re-emerge. Syed Abul Mansur Kamaluddin of the second story becomes a homeless ballad writer of Bengal and eventually meets ignoble death. Sir Cyril Ashley, one time a mighty colonial master, dies unattended and unnoticed in lonely circuit house in a remote corner of Bihar. All the characters in the last section of the novel suffer due to the devastating and disabling impact of partition on their life. All of a sudden, the country where they were born and bought up becomes an alien place. They feel out of place in their own country. This is what life holds out to these characters. The high and mighty all are crushed under the wheel of Time. Hyder writes philosophically: "Events are not important. Reality, myth and tradition all get mixed up. Historical time does not exist. The moment is eternal, man remains nameless. His creation gets lost in this ocean of eternity" (415-16).

Another interesting fact about the narrative design of the novel is that it has four stories whose similarity is only known to the readers, not to the characters in the novel.[4] The characters in different stories appear on the scene, enact their role and disappear, only the reader can recognize the common characters and recurrent pattern in these four stories. As there is no apparent connection between these stories, the reader tries to locate the connection at deeper levels. The reader eventually experiences the continuity of past in the present and a circular flow of time. Thus Hyder successfully and systematically manipulates the metaphor of river—Saryu, Padma, Gomti—to show the continuity of time from one historical epoch to the other.

In the course of narrative, Hyder emerges as an omniscient author to bring home the truth that the teller and the tale are inseparable. Her description of events from Indian history is not only accurate but also imaginatively rich. For instance:

> The Raja was an Urdu poet of Patna. He also happened to be the Naib Nazim of Bengal, Bihar and Orissa in Siraj-ud-Daula's Govt. When he heard of Siraj's defeat at Plassey the Raja spontaneously uttered this *sher,* then tore off his clothes and ran towards the forests. The Raja took sanyas and was never seen again. (230)

The following passage brilliantly underlines Hyder's imaginative treatment of Indian history:

> The U.P Govt. banned *Angaregy*. In 1935 Sajjad Zaheer and his comrades in London launched the Indian Progressive Writers Association, and its Manifesto was written by Dr. Jyoti Ghosh, Dr. Mulk Raj Anand, Promod Sen Gupta, Dr Muhammad Deen Taseer and Sajjad Zaheer.
>
> Calcutta, Lahore, Lucknow and the Muslim university, Aligarh, were among the major centres of Leftist activity.
>
> In 1937 two important things happened in Lucknow: the revival of the All India Muslim League and the establishment of Congress rule. According to Asad Mamoo the revival came about largely because of the personal rivalry between two local politicians, Choudhary Khaliq-uz Zaman and Syed Ali Zaheer. (231).

Besides this, many other historical events are recorded with rare insights into the psychology of the characters involved in these events. Some of the unforgettable events described by Hyder are: invasion of Chandragupta, the rise of the Mauryan Empire, the rise of Muslim rulers, the beginning of Mughal Empire, the East India Company and the expansion of British colonial rule in India, the forced abdication of Wajid Ali Shah in 1856, Sepoy Mutiny, seize of Lucknow Residency, the formation of Muslim League and so on. Hyder surpasses the historian in depicting the event and delineating the historical personages. One of the memorable scenes, described with rare ingenuity, is the counter Proclamation issued by Queen Hazrat Mahal.

Hyder's narrative is replete with divergent threads and it symbolically represents the composite culture of India. She liberally uses sufi songs, biography of Islamic saints, English nursery rhymes, Urdu couplets, world history, Eurasian jokes, and Indian art, aesthetics and philosophy. In each story there is an interplay of different literatures, languages and aesthetics. The first story mixes together different elements from Greek, Vedic, Buddhist and Persian cultures, the second familiarizes us with Islamic and British cultures; "the third and fourth stories explore the hybridization both of the British—from innkeeper to nabob—and the Indian—from feudal aristocracy to the colonial middle class."[5] The readers can feel the diversity of Indian culture while reading the novel. For instance, this Urdu couplet appropriately captures the mood of the 'moment.'

> Ghazalen, tum to waqif ho, kaho Majnun key marrey ki,
> Diwana mar gaya, aakhir ko, veeranay pe kya guzri. (230)
> (Gazelles of the desert! You know how Majnu died.
> What happened to the wilderness once he was gone?)

Hyder's narrative is made of a mosaic of fragmented and fractured narratives. The narrative does not follow a linear pattern. The four plots gradually dissolve into one but there are sudden jumps and jerks in the course of the narrative. It seems that Hyder follows the pattern of life and not that of poetics.

Hyder unfolds the felt experience of her characters through short narratives. She unfolds her story the way life unfolds its pattern. Human life does not follow any definite pattern and defies all laws of poetics. It is recalled and reconstructed in various ways through short and broken narratives. Perhaps Hyder believes that only fragmented stories can express the most delicate and difficult truths of life. It is through such stories that we feel a variety of human perceptions about society, history, time and reality.

In order to capture the very spirit of Indian culture, Hyder evokes the Indian way of story telling. In the chapter entitled

"Lala Rukh" she describes the manner in which a story is to be listened:

> "Lala Rukh," he resumed, "was Aurangzeb's daughter. She set forth in a caravan for Kashmir where she was to wed the King of Bokhara, and her barge sailed on the Indus. Say *hoon, hoon*, that is the tradition, when you listen to a story you keep saying *hoon*." (291)

The words/ phrases are not just simple Indian words. In Hyder's novel, they carry cultural moorings of Indian society. The readers enjoy the manner in which her English is imbued with Indian sensibility. This sensibility gets expressed through persona and places and the two are so closely linked with each other that one is unimaginable without the other. Note the following expression: "Life in the village is different. Here everyone is referred to as bhaiya, chacha, dada—a big self-contained joint-family, subdivided on the basis of caste" (229).

Hyder describes Kings, Queens, Nabobs, Princes and colonial masters with perfect verbal felicity. She uses the idiom appropriate to the status of her characters. This is how Hyder describes the conversation between Champa and Qamrun, the wife of the driver:

> "Bitiya you don't know what men are. We do. They are happy as long as you go on adoring them, and they want enormous sacrifices from us. . . .
>
> [Champa]: "He is not the only man in the world, there are thousands of others. All men are not alike, driver's wife," Champa said weakly. (267-68)

Her description of India, rather Indian subcontinent is not only historically correct but also culturally authentic in terms of minute details about people, places, customs, songs and superstitions. The descriptions are true to the minutest detail:

> So, how was this country to be defined? India was Qadeer's old mother, clad in yellow sari of rough cotton. She was a career woman, as it were, warder of the district jail's female wing. . . . The quiet avenues of Civil Lines where the dog-boys of the Angrez Sahebs took out their pets, were also India. In rural areas chicken-

> pox and small-pox were simply called "Mata" and considered a manifestation of the wrath of the goddess of Sitla. (226).

Like postmodern writers Hyder writes freely and mixes the literary genres to build a complex but convincing narrative web, as complex and convincing as human life is. The narrative is full of parables, legends, dreams, diaries, letters and chronicles.

River of Fire is a testimony to the fact that it is an outcome of Hyder's first-hand experience at various places wherever she happened to live. Unlike Salman Rushdie, who lived in India only in his childhood, and V.S Naipaul, who is oscillating between two heritages—Indian and Trinidadian, Hyder is genuinely cosmopolitan in her outlook as she has lived both in Pakistan and India. And she also lived in England while working for the B.B.C. She transcends the spatio-temporal boundaries and treats history as one living tradition and treats India and Pakistan as part of the large and unbroken civilization. At temporal level too there is an unbroken flow of time and it is evident from her artistic method which unfolds the history of Indian Subcontinent from 4 century B.C to the post-partition period. She may not have included in her narrative all the people and all the places as it is impossible in a book of fiction but she is absolutely conscious of this unbroken continuity both of time and history in her magnum opus *River of Time*.

But she has not received the kind of attention that she deserves. It may be because of late translation of her novel *River of Fire*. The work deserves a new method of reading i.e. a reading that reads from the point of view of the marginalized, the people on the periphery. This reading involves greater understanding of those things which have been deliberately excluded. Hyder does not write from the Eurocentric standpoint. She 'writes back' and writes from an alternative point of view. That is why her choice is Indian English not Babu English. Her prose in *River of Fire* is lyrical and yet draws elements from heterogeneous sources—legends, philosophy, diaries, letters, Urdu poetry, chronicles etc. The narrative is full of love, romance, intrigues, suspense, war and everything else which is essential for an interesting reading.

Of course, the reading of her novel requires a deeper understanding of the form and content of the Urdu novel. The canvas of her novel is full of royal personages—kings, queens, princes, colonial masters but she tells her story through the unprivileged voice—the voice coming from the periphery or somewhere between periphery and the centre.

To sum up, the beauty of *River of Fire* lies in its narrative art which captures the 'essence' of time from the ancient to the modern times. Nothing escapes her imaginative eyes as she goes on telling her tale which involves both involvement and detachment, and temporality and spatiality.

Nikhat Taj aptly remarks: "The imaginative universe of the novel knows no boundaries. The reader is transported to places and times which come alive with powerful immediacy. Q. Hyder has successfully achieved this effect in the *River of Fire* as a method. She captures systematically the very colour, drama, and excitement of the scene/event (in every section of the novel) as it unfolds in the pages of her narrative."[6]

NOTES

1 Qurratulain Hyder, *River of* Fire. New Delhi: Kali for Woman, 1998.

2 Peter Barry, *Beginning Theory: An Introduction to Literary and cultural Theory*, Manchester: Manchester Press, 1995. p.231

3 Gopi Chand Narang, "Qurratulain Hyder: An Author Par Excellence," *Indian Literature* 241 (Sept.-Oct., 2007), p.14.

4 Liyanage Amarakeerthi, "*River of Fire*: Critiquing the Ideology of History" http://www.urdustudies.com visited on 3.11.2009.

5 Kumkum Sangari, "Qurratulain Hyder's *Aag Ka Darya* http://www.museindia.com/showfocus3.asp?id=662 visited on 3.11.2009.p.12.

6 Nikhat Taj, "A Study of the Organising Principles in Qurratulain Hyder's *River of Fire*" *Indian Literature*, 252 (July-Aug. 2007), p. 209.

Narrative Technique in Chetan Bhagat's *The 3 Mistakes of My Life*

PRIYANKA LAMBA

We have not come across any advertisement of Chetan Bhagat's novels on the television, on roadside billboards or in newspapers. Neither is he prescribed in any university nor does he grace many literary functions. And yet he is what *The New York Times* says, "the biggest selling English language novelist in India's history." *The International Herald Tribune* has rightly praised Chetan Bhagat as a writer, "who has touched a nerve with young Indian readers and acquired almost cult status." What could be the possible reason for his selling more than a daily newspaper? Apart from the theme, his narrative style too holds the key to his immense popularity. Bhagat, in his novels, creates simple characters with whom any young Indian can identify, and puts them in situations which again are faced by everybody in day-to-day life. Added to this is the simple and lucid expression which immediately strikes a chord with the readers.

I have chosen Bhagat's third novel *The 3 Mistakes of My Life* for a critical evaluation of his narrative style. What *India Today* commented about Chetan Bhagat's first novel *Five Point Someone* can very well be applied to *The 3 Mistakes of My Life*—a "well constructed book with great characters and a captivating plot. Definitely on the right side of five-point something on the 10 point scale." Chetan Bhagat has integrated the facts and events with the imaginative life of three youngsters—Govind, Ish and Omi. The novel is a personal memoir of the narrator Govind who confesses to the author the three mistakes he made in his life. As a consequence of these mistakes, he is forced to attempt suicide. Chetan Bhagat gets an email which is "a combined suicide note and a confession letter" (1) from Govind "an ordinary boy in Ahmedabad" (prologue).

The complete title of the novel is *The 3 Mistakes of My Life—A Story about Business, Cricket and Religion.* As in his other novels, this title also has a number in it—3. When asked about it Chetan replied, "I am a banker, I can't get numbers out of my head." Cricket, the nation's game, cricket fever, small town politics, earthquake, religious riots and first love—all these are intermingled in the lives of three teenagers living in Ahmedabad of the early 2000 A.D. The writer has liberally used the names of famous cricketers like Tendulkar, Kumble, Ganguly, Dravid, Adam Gilchrist and others and dates of the matches between India and Australia to lend the story an illusion of reality. Cricket in India is a worshipped game and the cricketers are idolized by the Indians. Bhagat has portrayed this relationship between cricket and religion by naming his main players Govind, Ish and Omi after gods. And their cricket shop Team India Cricket Shop is opened "right inside the Swami temple complex. Next to the flower and puja shops" (16). This relationship is encashed by the businessman Govind and this is probably suggested by the title itself. The three main characters represent the three fibres of the story—Govind is a businessman, Ish is an ardent cricket lover and Omi is a religious boy—which are woven together to make a beautiful fabric.

The plot of the novel can be compared with a cricket match. Bhagat's style of telling it as a background story involving himself forms the pitch of the novel. The email from Govind makes him come to Ahmedabad and listen to the commentary of the match through the eyes of Govind. The first player is Gopi (Govind) who is a typical Gujarati businessman belonging to "Navaldharis, a hardcore entrepreneur community in Gujarat. Everyone there does a business" (110). He and his mother eke out their living by running a Gujarati snack business and by giving tuitions in Maths. Ish is the second player who is an avid cricket lover and whose passion lies in playing, teaching and watching cricket. He is the son of a stereotype grumpy Indian dad who taunts him on account of his failures all the time. The third player is Omi who is not as talented as his other two friends are but is dedicated to them. He is the son of the Swamibhakt temple priest but has no desire to follow in his father's footsteps. One of the bowlers is Ali Nasser, the son of a Muslim politician. He is a twelve-year old wonder-kid who has the specialty of hitting sixes. His fame attracts Gopi and Ish who end up coaching him in cricket and Maths. He takes the wicket of Omi who dies while saving Ali during the Gujarat riots. The second bowler is Vidya, Ish's sister and a Maths-hater. She has to study because she wants to study in Mumbai and that is her ticket to escape her parents. She takes tuition from Govind and quite predictably makes Govind break the protocol of "never ever hit on your best friend's sister" (172). She thus bowls out the friendship of Gopi and Ish. The third bowler is Bittoo Mama, Omi's uncle who symbolizes the older generation of Hindus that constantly criticizes the younger generation for not being politically involved in religion. It is his religious fervor which brings tragedy in the life of Ish, Gopi and Omi.

These players also had to fight against the odds brought in the wake of real incidents that rocked India during the period 1999 to 2002—the severest earthquake, the Godhra incident and the worst of communal riots. Gopi, Ish and Omi opened their 'Team India Cricket' shop in April 2000. The ordinary 20 x 10 feet space soon becomes their refuge and their success story. The first odd hits them in January 2001 when the Bhuj earthquake reduces to rubble the Navrangpura Mall. It is here that Govind had invested money in a new shop. This calamity throws them in debt.

For them a miracle happens after this disaster. India wins against Australia in March 2001, making their cricket business soar. Six months later, a terrorist attack happens in the USA which fuels religious tension in Gujarat. The players face another odd in Feb. 2002, when the Ayodhya-bound Sabarmati Express is set on fire at Godhra railway station. In this, Bittoo Mama's son is killed. Bloody sectarian riots follow. Bittoo Mama wants Ali's blood as a revenge for his son's death. In a dramatic bloody situation, Ali, Ish and Gopi are injured and ironically Omi, the next generation Hindu leader dies while saving the Muslim boy

Ali. Everybody now seems to have lost the match. It is here that umpire Chetan Bhagat steps in to give the novel a happy ending. Ish and Gopi are reconciled, Ali undergoes a surgery and his batting talent is restored. Vidya goes to Mumbai to study PR.

Thus, Chetan Bhagat has woven fact and fiction in his novel. People, especially the youth feel as if it is their story. Chetan Bhagat, through the personal involvement of Govind, Ish and Omi in the Gujarat earthquake, Godhra incident followed by the communal riots narrates the horrors faced by the innocent people of Gujarat. The violence that erupted in the innocent lives of these three friends symbolizes what happened in the real life of the people of Gujarat. The author has used an ironic tone to tear asunder the mask of hypocrisy, callousness and false morality of the Indians. For instance, when India is losing a match, Omi comments "The Khakra's crispy." He is chided by Ish for his shallow sensory pleasure in a moment of national grief" (2). At another place, Bhagat describes 26 January as a happy day for Indians because "Whether or not you feel patriotic, it is a guaranteed holiday in the first month of the year" (104). Playing down the destruction that happened in Ahmedabad the news channels report, "Compared to Gujarat, Ahmedabad had better luck. The new city lost only fifty multi-storey buildings. They said only a few hundred people died in Ahmedabad compared to tens of thousands elsewhere. It is funny when hundreds of people dying is tagged with 'only.' Each of those people would have had families, and hopes and aspirations all shattered in forty-five seconds. But that is how maths works—compared to thirty thousand, hundreds is a rounding error" (110).

Each character reflects his or her personality and taste through the use of phrases and similes. As Vidya, Ish's sister and a student of science, while commenting on the friendship of Ish, Omi and Gopi, says, "You, Ish and Omi are really close. Like you have known each other since you were sperm." Similarly Gopi, a mathematician describes the talkative nature of girls in mathematical terms, "Girls talk in circles. Like an algebra problem, it takes a few steps to get them to the point" (89). This use of registers of different subjects adds a tinge of humour to the language. This is evident on almost every page of the book. Even the passionate scenes are spiced up with humour. In the kissing scene between Govind and Vidya, romance is mixed with realty which is quite humorous: "Her lips were eight millimeters apart from mine, soon the gap reduced to zero. We kissed again. The mosquitoes on our respective heads rejoined. We broke away from each other because even passionate people need oxygen" (184).

Corresponding to the context, content and the linear narrative is the language which is simple and colloquial. Chetan Bhagat has been criticized for his simple style and I would defend him by quoting him only, "I think a writer's first job is to strike a chord and not please the elitist circles. It can't be just the language, as it is simply the common language of the people. It is more about what is being said and communicated that strikes a chord." (Interview, *Hindustan Times*, 28 July, 2008)

The selection of Ahmedabad, a simple town of Gujarat, as the setting of the novel also smells of the author's nostalgia about the place from where he did his MBA and where he met his wife. The author on the one hand exhibits an absolute fidelity to the reality of life and on the other hand gives cinematic/dramatic touch to the story. In this, we find sentiment, romance, love, business, religion, action and of course, cricket. The juiciness and the dramatic events of the novel have made it suitable for a film script and prompted Farhan Akhtar and Abhishek Kapoor to turn the novel into a film.

Indeed, Chetan Bhagat is a phenomenon that has affected everyone. He is a successful writer who will divide the Indian publishing scenario into pre- and post-Bhagat eras. Among other things the novel contains a true picture of the anxieties, struggles and life of youth of contemporary India, the developments of recent past, through imaginatively realized characters in an artistically conceived plot.

Work Cited

Bhagat, Chetan. *The 3 Mistakes of My Life*. New Delhi: Rupa, 2008

Amitav Ghosh's *The Shadow Lines*: A Study in Dialogic Art

NARINDER KUMAR SAINI

Among the twentieth century Indian English novelists influenced by modern techniques, Amitav Ghosh emerges as a remarkable novelist for his untiring experiments in his novels. *The Shadow Lines*, the masterpiece of Amitav Ghosh, employs the modern styles of novel writing vividly. The singular modern stylistic which seems to best epitomize Ghosh's *The Shadow Lines* is the novelist's dexterous use of dialogic imagination in his masterpiece.

Dialogic Criticism owes its origin to the critical principles of Mikhail Bakhtin, the best-known Russian critic of the 20th century. To Bakhtin a literary work is not a text whose meanings are produced by the play of impersonal linguistic or economic or cultural forces, but a site for the dialogic interaction of multiple voices. In his famous book *Problems of Dostoevsky's Poetics*, he contrasts the monologic novels of Tolstoy with 'dialogic' or 'polyphonic' novels of Dostoevsky. Bakhtin says that in Dostoevsky's novels, characters are liberated to speak "a plurality of independent and unmerged voices and consciousnesses, a genuine polyphony of fully valid voices" (Abrams 73). Examined in the light of these perceptions, in *The Shadow Lines* the narrations of the interaction among characters are 'double-voiced,' 'multiple,' 'ironic' or 'polyphonic.'

The very narrative of *The Shadow Lines* deals with the author's vision of life which is marked by irony and indeterminacy. Tridib, the protagonist of the novel always thinks beyond frontier limits which are arbitrarily drawn on maps. But then the protagonist desired to live beyond the man-made, arbitrarily drawn maps of geographical limits into a romantic, complex, universal human relationships, called 'mirror' where love, beauty, humanity abound. Ironically, his whole life remained a conflict, a desire built around wish-fulfilment. The narrator recognizes in Tridev's desire a deep imagination for a space without history, a timeless world beyond practical reason. Hence the aesthetic forte of the novel lies in the conflict between two images—maps and mirrors. It seems that the unending conflict between the two lends the novel an expanse beyond mimetic realism to incorporate the elements of mystery, and irony of existence. Hence the narratives of the novel focus on the unfinalized and unfinalisable crisis arising from the complex vision of the protagonist which gives the novel dialogic dimension. While in England, Tridib loved the English girl May, but then the failure in love due to racial differences added to the enigma, dilemma and pathos of Tridib's existence. His desire for love of man and woman beyond time and space of history and geography remains insatiable to the end. His reference to the myth of Tristan and Iseult reinforces the never-ending pathos and frustration of love among lovers belonging to different nationalities. The narrator says:

> It happened everywhere, wherever you wish it. It was an old story, the best story in Europe, . . . when Europe was a better place, a place without borders and countries—it was a German story. . . . It was the story of a hero called Tristan, a very sad story, about a man without a country, who fell in love with a woman-across-the-seas. (186)

The plot of the whole novel issues forth from dialogic intercourse between the present persona and Tridib (the persona's uncle). It seems that the persona's memorization and recollection of the past events shared with him by his late uncle regarding cross-border discriminations and intra-national communal riots constitutes the chief subject-matter of the novel. Thanks to the profound imagination of the persona, the whole past is available to him endlessly. The unbroken continuing and unified consciousness of the persona enable him to communicate his complex vision of life. In other words, Ghosh's protagonist, like those of Joyce, Woolf, Dostoevsky and James, is capable of interweaving past, present and future like a stream of consciousness. Much of the narrative is dialogic, rather than monologic as it is dramatic, interactive and pluralistic. The real desire of the persona is an unfailing dialogue between physical and metaphysical, mundane and primitive. But then the curiously cosmopolitan persona is out to obliterate any barrier or border, physical or emotional. The persona expresses his deep urge vividly which has dialogic signification:

> And still, I knew that the sights Tridib saw in his imagination were infinitely more detailed, more precise than anything I would ever see. He said to me once that one could never know anything except through desire, real desire, which was not the same thing as greed or lust; a pure, painful and primitive desire, a longing for everything that was not oneself, a torment or the flesh, that carried one beyond the limits of one's mind to other times and other places, and even, if one was lucky, to a place where there was no border between oneself and one's image in the mirror. (29)

The central crisis of postcolonial era i.e. border crisis and separation anxiety with which the novel begins remains unresolved almost throughout the novel. The novelist ironically laughs at only partial, physical and casual pleasure of people belonging to different nationalities and races. The relationship between Tridib and May remains merely physical and fails to fructify into intimate matrimonial alliance. Ironically, Tridib returns to India and during a communal riot in Calcutta, he is killed. But then this vicious cycle of angst, anxiety, victimization and frustration of the protagonist continues and is carried forward through the narrator of the novel. In a sense, he is the alter-ago of the protagonist. Sadly enough, he is deceived by fanciful physical embrace of the same British woman (May). Consciously, the persona is victimized by May and their so-called suggestion of unresolved crisis of life. The novelist vividly hints at it: "I stayed, and when we lay in each others' arms quietly, in the night, I could tell that she was glad, and I was glad too, and grateful, for the glimpse she had given me of a final redemptive mystery" (252).

As it ends, so it begins with puzzling problem of a postcolonial world. The postcolonial issues raised by the narrator remain insoluble and the novel remains an open-ended discourse. There is something inconclusive and unfinalisable about the novel which has made it a postmodern work. *The Shadow Lines* appears to be a study in dialogic art as it includes variety of complex issues pertaining to society, country and the world. The novel is, for the most part, an extremely self-conscious meditation on the themes of nationality, internationality, cultural and historical self-determination, as also on the enormously conflicted transition from the temporary certitudes of the nationalist freedom struggle to the disillusions and discontents that have marked India as an independent state. As we might expect, or rather, as we have learnt to expect from the place of women in colonial and postcolonial Indian society, the weight of sexual and cultural definition is borne unequally by men and women, with men as the putative agents of socio-subjects. Women—Ila in particular, but also Tha'mma and May—are represented as carrying the greatest burden of historical dislocation, and it is their 'missteps that lead to personal tragedy, as also trace the rocky paths of larger national and international conflicts. The novel offers a radical critique of political boundaries, vaporizing their rigidities into shadow-lines, but its account of the relationship between women and culture is less hopeful—for them there are no transformations of cultural frontiers, only inelegant transgressions.

The dialogic imagination of Amitav Ghosh enables him to make the vast use of esthetic elements into artistic harmony and coherence. In *The Shadow Lines*, it is, of course the male narrator's growing imagination, empathy and intellectuality which allow for the exploration and understanding of complex themes. As his horizons expand and become international in scope, his questions, memories and experiences provide the structure of the narrative. But even as his consciousness mediates and frames other voices, stories and experiences, we become aware that some of these voices counterpoint his narrative, and even interrogate his telling of the story. The narrative of this novel, not unlike the process of sub-continental independence, engenders and empowers political subjects unequally, and indeed represents them asymmetrically. *The Shadow Lines* becomes not simply a male bildungsroman, an authorized autobiography, with its obvious agendas and priorities, but also a dialogic, more open-ended, telling of the difficult interdependencies and inequalities that compose any biography of a nation.

It seems that the novelist brings about the blending of diverse and dual elements into *The Shadow Lines*. Significantly, Ghosh reverses the usual gender attribution of the qualities 'active-passive.' It is the male characters who exemplify passive attitudes, and the women who are figures of action. Both terms are revaluated as modes of existence, i.e. way of living. The discriminations that are made in the process may be viewed as the most radical aspect of the moral issues explored in this novel. The central male characters in *The Shadow Lines* are the narrator, his cousin Tridib, and Nick Price, all of whom may be described as 'passive' by nature. The chief women characters are the narrator's grandmother, his cousin Ila, and May Price, whom I shall call 'active,' in contrast to the men in the novel.

There is, first of all, an explicit contrast between the cultural rootedness of the passive male protagonists and the migrancy of the women. Both Tridib and the narrator 'belong'—not just to their native Calcutta milieu but to the 'world' itself. Of his family, Tridib alone, we are told, lives in Calcutta, occupying the large family mansion with his old grandmother, while his diplomat father and brother and their families move around the world. From this vantage point of 'belonging,' both also have the freedom to range through geography and history, which are their vivid constructs of knowledge and imagination.

One of the chief loci of value in *The Shadow Lines* is the visual imagination: "Tridib was an archaeologist, he was not interested in fairylands: the one thing he wanted to teach me, he used to say, was to use my imagination with precision" (29). The viewer's exercise of memory and imagination enable him to 'see' in the mind's eye, more vividly than in actuality: "The sights Tridib saw in his imagination were infinitely more detailed, more precise than anything I would ever see. [. . .] Desire [. . .] carried one beyond the limits of one's mind to other times and other places" (29). This is a gift that can be trained and cultivated: "I puzzled over what Tridib had said, and in a while I began to imagine the sloping roofs of Colombo for myself: the pattern they made if one wheeled in the sky above them, how sharply they rose if one looked at them from below, the mossiness of their tiles when one saw them close up, from a first floor window" (29). Tridib represents the ideal mode of being-in-the-world with the narrator aspiring to it.

In the final analysis, *The Shadow Lines* is a dialogic text imbedded in social, economic, political and ideological systems of the day. The novel emerges as dialogic in its inclusion of heterogeneous elements which give the novel an open-ended implication beyond the words-on-the-page form.

Works Cited

Ghosh, Amitav. *The Shadow Lines*. New Delhi: Oxford, 1988.

Mikhail Bakhtin. *Problems of Dostoevsky's Poetics*, 1929. Ed. and trans. Caryl Emerson. Minneapolis: University of Minnesota Press, 1984.

Treatment of Time and Order in Arundhati Roy's *The God of Small Things*

URVASHI PRABHAT

Whereas real life cannot escape the tethers of the laws of time which are beyond the purview of human influence, the narrative act can well defy the overpowering sway of time: blurring the boundaries between the present, past and the future; living some events for a seemingly unending duration of time, while others spanning several years in real time are jumped over in the most natural manner. It is creative privilege that impossible chronologies are created wherein the natural order of happenings is inverted in more than one way, the narration begins in *media res* and is dotted with gaps, and some events are repeated while others are 'understood' to have occurred though never overtly stated in the narration.

The narratology in *The God of Small Things* throws the reader into a time machine: beginning in the present time, which moves back by almost twenty three years within a span of two pages and a half. Characters that are thirty one years old today suddenly revert to a stage where they are still to be born and yet again to seven years later within the next two fifty words. This time shift and time scramble is not without a plan. Right at the outset of the narration it establishes firmly the relationship between Estha and Rahel, the twins: one which defies the tyranny of time—'They had known each other before Life began.' The umbilical connection is not one way for the 'Dizygotic' (2) twins but it is actually two-way. The past, present, and the future are brought into fine synthesis to intersperse the narration with the feeling of the failure of time for once to alter their bonding till it finally assumes the intimacy with which 'Life' began for them.

Similarly, Ricoeur observes that a narrative organizes time as "a pattern from a succession":

> Every narrative combines two dimensions in various proportions, one chronological and the other non-chronological. The first may be called the episodic dimension, which characterizes the story as made out of events. The second is the configurational dimension, according to which the plot construes significant wholes out of scattered events. Here I am borrowing from Louis O. Mink the notion of a configurational act, which he interprets as a "grasping together." I understand this act to be the act of plot, as eliciting a pattern from a succession. (178)

The philosophy of time as 'an agent that heals' is reverted in the novel and encourages the reader to look at time from a new dimension. The writer does not shift blocks of time in the flashback or montage technique for long periods. The narrative technique at work is that of stream of consciousness where the past intermittently exists with the present. Though meeting after twenty-three years, Estha and Rahel's pain is made more poignant rather than dulled with the passage of time, pushing them inevitably into breaking a 'Love Law' that was once before broken with terribly tragic consequences. It was the law 'That lay down who should be loved. And how. And how much.' (328). Breaking these laws is the worst of taboos, and those that break them are brutally punished. Desire and desperation, though, overcome the 'Love Laws' at key moments in the novel. Thus, they stride across the time barrier of the years they have lived to relive the umbilical connection, committing the unspeakable act It is another matter though that when the Law was broken earlier, it was to revel in happiness: not, as in their case, to share in 'hideous grief.'

According to Gerard Genette, episodes in a narrative which defy chronology (whether by narration before they actually occur or after) can be designated as "anachronies" and those that follow natural time sequencing as the "first narrative." In reality, of course, events ought to have occurred sequentially but are rendered anachronically in the narrative to evoke in the reader the query "How did it happen?" and "What caused it?" rather than

"What happened next?" The incestuous act of Estha and Rahel is a means to mitigate the abject misery that spans the thirty-one years of their lives. Thus the almost refrain like "They had known each other before Life began," or Estha and Rahel's perception of themselves "together as Me, and separately, individually, as We or Us" (2) are actually instances of Completing Prolepses which Genette defines as a foreshadowing which fills a later gap ahead of time. This prolepsis, Genette says, has a "reach" (the measure of time between the first narrative where it is introduced and the time of the anachrony) and an "extent" (the duration of the analepsis or prolepsis).

It is in order to emphasize upon the events that led up to the story, that the consequences and the characters themselves build on that Roy has structured the novel non-sequentially. It allows the author optimum flexibility to selectively develop the happenings and the themes which she chooses to, subtly preparing the reader for a point of view which is actually the children's (though more of Rahel's than Estha's), blaming, with them, the events of and prior to the preceding twenty three years for the climax. Thus the kaleidoscopic presentation, the interspersing of long syntactical structures with notably short ones, the alternating of ideas striking for their very profundity with almost silly, non words characteristic of children's thought process (and hence their typical speech) are all well thought out devices contributing to the whole. It firmly establishes the bitter fact that for the children, time has at once frozen and sped forward, as if past and present are mere moments and not entities that can be accounted for in terms of minutes, hours, days and years:

> Edges, Borders, Boundaries, Brinks and Limits have appeared like a team of trolls on their separate horizons. Short creatures with long shadows, patrolling the Blurry End. Gentle half moons have gathered under their eyes and they are as old as Ammu was when she died. Thirty-one.
> Not old.
> Not Young.
> But a viable die-able age. (3)
> . . . the Ayemenem house still had a river sense.

> A rushing, rolling, fishswimming sense. (30)
> Sophie Mol.
> Thimble-drinker
> Coffin-cartwheeler. (135)
> Little Girls Playing.
> Sweet
> One beach-colored.
> One brown.
> One Loved.
> One Loved a Little Less. (186)
> They lay like that for a long time. Awake in the dark. Quietness and Emptiness.
> Not old. Not young.
> But a viable die-able age. (327)

Traditionally, stylisticians differentiate between content and style as the distinction between 'what-one-has-to-say' and 'how-one-says-it' (Leech and Short 38). Applied to narratology in literature, it is the difference between the story and discourse, i.e. between 'what-is-told' and 'how-it's-transmitted.' The latter would signify much more than langue (the language system): it would rather be more appropriate to attribute the meaning of 'how-it's-transmitted' to parole (defined as 'an oral utterance: word of mouth,' *Universal Dictionary*, Reader's Digest). In *The God of Small Things,* the narrative follows a circular design: events race backwards into the past to traverse decades and then, just as abruptly, revert to the present: lack of order and time as seen from the vantage of the children gives the narrative its particular flavour, explaining the interspersing of the narration with 'children's vocabulary,' they being the third person (though only implicitly) narrating the story.

As we lift a few layers of the narratology, however, and attempt to clear the mist of disorderly arrangement of time in the novel, the code of the underlying motifs which are a recurring and constant feature of the content, reveals itself. Love, discovery and loss of it, shortcomings of the prevailing social system to provide an effective cushion to victims of unrequited love, and the larger inability of humanity to recognize and accept that which lies on the extremes of the social or emotional spectrum:

the myriad tragedies of the Ipe family (and more of the extended Ipe family) are conveyed through the medium of the disjointed, jigsaw-pieces-put-together parole of seven or thirty one year olds: Estha and Rahel. Typically, like the round song that children sing: Round and round the mulberry bush: the story adopts a circular route; beginning with the arrival of Rahel at their ancestral house in Ayemenem, tracing the course of hers, Estha's and Ammu's lives twenty three years ago, going on to explore a few more years that Ammu lived, and finally completing the circle by drawing the tragic parallel between the now grown up Estha and Rahel's present and Ammu's lives. It is interesting that in this arrangement of events, the years that elapse after Ammu's death till Rahel's return seem to have little significance and are, consequently, given little print space. Even the 'climax' when it comes, is grossly understated: as if there was little to be said, one being prepared for it since the very beginning. "physically separate, but with joint entities" (2).

This is again alternated with the transgression of Ammu decades ago. The inevitable parallel has been drawn. The present and the past appear as consecutively occurring moments, flouting the natural, linear chronological order of time as experienced in reality. In real life we do not have the liberty to go forward or backward in time no matter how much we wanted to, time being a merciless fiend that can not be manipulated. But in *The God of Small Things*, the perception of time itself is altered, diminishing the traditional, familiar experience of it. It brings to light the hidden meaning of time, unifying all experience into a single moment, reinforcing the philosophy that even if the flame of 'life' as opposed to 'existence' flickers for the shortest fraction of time, it is still worthy of being cherished as a rare treasure.

Works Cited

Leech, Geoffrey N. and Michael H. Short. *Style in Fiction*. London: Longman, 1981.

Ricoeur, Paul. "Narrative Time" *Critical Inquiry*, Vol. 7, No. I on Narrative (Autumn, 1980), pp. 169-90.

Genette, Gerard. *Narrative Discourse: An Essay in Method.* Trans. Jane E. Lewin. Ithaca: Cornell University Press, 1980.

Woodman, Leonara. "A Linguistic Approach to Prose Style," *The English Journal*, Vol. 62, No. 4 (Apr., 1973), pp. 587-590+599-603.

Judy, Stephen. "Style and the Teaching of Literature and Composition," *The English Journal*, Vol. 56, No. 2 (Feb., 1967), pp. 281-85.

Jhumpa Lahiri's Style of Writing in *Interpreter of Maladies*

SHILPI AHUJA

"Jhumpa Lahiri is the kind of writer who makes you want to grab the next person you see and say 'Read this!' Lahiri is a dazzling storyteller with a distinct voice, an eye for nuance and an ear for irony. She is one of the finest short story writers I've read." These words by Amy Tan have also been echoed by several critics who find Lahiri's art of writing fiction simply extraordinary.

The purpose of my paper is to study the style of Jhumpa Lahiri Vourvoulias (born Nilanjana Sudeshna) in her collection of short-stories titled *Interpreter of Maladies* (1999). It won the 2000 Pulitzer Prize for fiction and the Hemingway Foundation/PEN Award. It was also chosen as *The New Yorker*'s Best Debut of the year. As a collection of nine distinct short stories, this debut work addresses sensitive dilemmas in the lives of Indians or Indian immigrants. The themes of these stories include marital difficulties, miscarriages, and the disconnection between first and second generation immigrants in the United States. The stories are set in the north-eastern United States, and in India, particularly Calcutta. The stories are "on-the-face" direct and embrace you in their warm folds without you even being aware of it. She has helped in throwing clearer light on an Indian's perspective of life in an alien land. However, the book doesn't reek of ethnocentricity—it has a universal flavour and appeal that an immigrant from any corner of the world would be able to relate to.

Lahiri writes about the Indian immigrant experience in America. Her style comprises of eloquent language which clothes mature observations and delicate insights, all of which give a lie to her age. Her writing is smooth-flowing and gentle and has a universal flavour and appeal. Her style is simple yet smart, sparing in words yet divinely eloquent, weaving visual images for her reader in a startlingly realistic manner. What is remarkable is that her stories are a mix of sensitivity and thought-provoking at one fell swoop.

All the nine stories in *Interpreter of Maladies* focus on the characters' inability to communicate with people who are important in their lives. These stories are—"A Temporary Matter," "When Mr. Pirzada Came to Dine," "Interpreter of Maladies," "A Real Durwan," "Sexy," "Mrs. Sen's," "This Blessed House," "The Treatment of Bibi Haldar," and "The Third and Final Continent."

Teeming with all manner of humanity, it is in turn frank and subtle, bold and understated. Jhumpa Lahiri's style explores Indianness in all her stories regardless of wherever they are set. She has developed multicultural perspectives through her writings. Her work revolves around the themes of isolation and loss; issue of marriage; marital difficulties, with the characters trying to maintain the traditional family values.

Lahiri is able to demonstrate her point in writing by merely mentioning the issue that a character is facing. This is a technique that is present in much of her fiction. She is able to draw her readers into the story not only through her detail but also by making them feel the emotional, physical and mental needs of the characters.

What is remarkable about her is that although she has never been an immigrant, she is able to step into the latter's shoes without a stumble or a shoe-bite. Call it uncanny or intuitive but one cannot ignore the fact that she has a gift for tucking away memories and observations in the back of her literary mind and churning them into a mixture of sensitive and thought-provoking stories.

The anthology has three stories previously published in *The New Yorker*, plus six previously unpublished works. The stories all draw upon different aspects of her Indian background. Each one of the stories is affected in some way or another by India. Some of the stories take place in India; others involve the lives of Indian immigrants in the United States. The bulk of the stories, though, are about second generation Indian-Americans, like Lahiri herself. *Interpreter of Maladies* is redolent of India itself. Teeming with all manner of humanity, it is in turn frank and subtle, bold and understated. There is an immediacy to her style that bridges any gulfs between the more structured traditions of Indian culture and the brashness of American life.

All the stories in *Interpreter of Maladies* focus on the characters' inability to communicate with people who are important in their lives. She continues her story by plotting her "motif of exclusion, loneliness, and search for fulfillment" as the central issue.

Another impressive aspect of Lahiri's writing is her ability to write in the voices of both genders. On writing from the male perspective, she says, in an interview in the Houghton Mifflin Books online "Reader's Guide," "It was an exhilarating and liberating thing to do . . . . It's a challenge, as well. I always have to ask myself, would a man think this? do this?" This method of narration gives her the ability to balance the gender representation in her book.

> He did not know what he would do or say to Mrs. Das once they arrived at the hills. Perhaps he would tell her what a pleasing smile she had. Perhaps he would compliment her strawberry shirt, which he found irresistibly becoming. Perhaps, when Mr. Das was busy taking a picture, he would take her hand. (60)

Interpreter of Maladies is an excellent example of the fact that ethnic literature can encompass universal themes and experiences while still drawing attention to the history and culture of a specific group of people. The stories of her first book whisper and scream traces of India through the details of the characters who become fictional testaments to the 'complex and conflicted world of Indian immigrants in the United States.'

> Sanjeev went to the bathroom to throw away the ashes. The cigarette butt still bobbed in the toilet bowl, but the tank was refilling,

> so he had to wait a moment before he could flush it again. In the mirror of the medicine cabinet he inspected his long eyelashes—like a girl's, Twinkle liked to tease. (140)

The impulse that courses through *Interpreter of Maladies* might be called the ardour of empathy. In the nine stories that make up this collection, she displays a steadfast curiosity about human behaviour and a healthy respect for its mystery. Shrewd but not judgmental, she has the grace to make us feel close even to foolishness and timidity and the wit to make actions logical without being predictable. *The Hindustan Times* comments, "There is magic in the way Jhumpa Lahiri weaves her nine tales. Lahiri's choice of subjects is exemplary, her keenness of observations astonishing, and her style taunt and sincere."

Her debut story collection explores issues of love and identity among immigrants and cultural transplants. With a compelling, universal fluency, she portrays the practical and emotional adversities of her diverse characters in elegant and direct prose. Whether describing hardships of a lonely Indian wife adapting to life in the United States or illuminating the secret pain of a young couple as they discuss their betrayals during a series of electrical blackouts, her bittersweet stories avoid sentimentality without abandoning compassion. "But nothing was pushing Shukumar. Instead he thought of how he and Shobha had become experts at avoiding each other in their three-bedroom house, spending as much time on separate floors as possible." (4)

One of the themes she deals in most prolifically is the search for identity, as defined by the self, by others, by location and by circumstance. In her stories, everything—including gender, homeland, geography, occupation, and role within the community—can act in determining and qualifying identity. She brings up interesting questions as to what can and cannot act as agents in the determination of identity.

The *Book Magazine* states, "There is not one false note here, not one misstep or hesitation . . . . Each of these nine stories has the capacity to amaze us. . . . In Lahiri's sympathetic tales, the pang of disappointment turns into a sudden hunger to know more. . . . She breathes unpredictable life into the page, and the reader finishes each story re-seduced, wishing he could spend a whole novel with its characters. There is nothing accidental about her success; her plots are as elegantly constructed as a fine proof in mathematics. Lahiri is 'wow.' "

Lahiri deals greatly in generalizations of gender roles in *Interpreter of Maladies*; many of her characters depicted in diasporic situations hold onto role definitions that American readers find stereotypical of Indian culture. Such generalizations (and the sometimes-ironic reversals of them) act as literary tools that add to her most sympathetic characters and her most poignant storylines. *Interpreter of Maladies* takes us beyond our own imaginations and we are all the better for it.

From the foregoing analysis, we can summarise that the Pulitzer has endorsed the cultural glamorization of both Lahiri and the version of India in America she is supposed to represent. Hence the feel the reviews and interviews give: there is a closed set of interpretive possibilities surrounding her *Interpreter of Maladies*. The stories are about Indian culture, because the characters are Indians, Indians in America, or Indian-Americans, never Americans or never about Americans.

> The next day, when Dev came to visit, Miranda asked him what his wife looked like. She was nervous to ask, waiting until he'd smoked the last of his cigarettes, crushing it with a firm twist into the saucer. She wondered if they'd quarrel. But Dev wasn't surprised by the question. He told her, spreading some smoked whitefish on a cracker, that his wife resembled an actress in Bombay named Madhuri Dixit. (98)

This critical myopia reveals the limits of "official multiculturalism"—a practice that celebrates diversity at the same time that it reifies minority or ethnic writers and their art into always hyphenated, always cultural, always identitarian representatives served up for mainstream America's consumption.

Thus, with each story, she draws believable characters in both ordinary and extraordinary situations, making the task seem sweetly effortless in the process. The range of her style, talent and imagination is broad but she never loses focus in its execution. She has the unique ability to paint the worlds of both the immigrant and the native in miniature, allowing for immersion in detail while simultaneously placing them in a grand, sweeping perspective of universal truth. She remains one of the most promising young talents. Unlike many contemporaries who have won quick renown, she does not strive for cleverness, or promote quirky ventures for their sheer novelty. Nor does she peddle personal tragedy, hipness or exoticism, let alone insulate herself with alternating blasts of irony and earnestness: "As he watched the couple the room went dark, and he spun around. Shobha had turned the lights off. She came back to the table and sat down, and after a moment Shukumar joined her. They wept together, for the things they now knew." (22)

Last but not the least, the most important aspect of Lahiri's style is the use of simple language; detailed insight of her characters; themes having universal appeal; provoking readers to think "what next"; simplicity and down-to-earth approach—undoubtedly caters as well as appeals to the common man of yesterday, today and tomorrow.

Works Cited

Lahiri, Jhumpa. *Interpreter of Maladies*. Noida: HarperCollins, 1999, Reprint 2005.

Kipen, David. "Interpreting Indian Culture with Stories." Rev. of *Interpreter of Maladies*, by Jhumpa Lahiri. *San Francisco Chronicle* SF Gate 25 June 1999: E-1. 13 Feb 2006 <http://www.sfgate.com/cgi-bin/article.cgi?f=/c/a/1999/06/24/ DD49368.DTL&hw= interpreter+of+maladies&sn=001&sc= 1000>.

Sarangi, Jaydeep. "The Enigma of Cultural Multiplicity: a Study of *Interpreter of Maladies*." *Jhumpa Lahiri, the Master Storyteller: A Critical Response to "Interpreter of Maladies,"* ed. Suman Bala. New Delhi: Khosla, 2002. 116-21.

Ruth P. Jhabvala's *Heat and Dust*: A Study in Narratology

SUMITA ASHRI

Ruth Prawer Jhabvala has been unduly criticized and uncritically appreciated, both in India and abroad, for her subject matter as well as for her stylistic paraphernalia. The handling and treatment of the highly sensitive issues like stereotyped-joint-family system, arranged marriages, romantic and extra-marital love affairs, children and parents, divorce and the keeping of mistresses by the elite class, where even angels fear to tread, has generated both heat and dust. For example, there has been a very common approach to the expiation and appreciation of the central concerns of Jhabvala in *Heat and Dust* in terms of the invasion of the West into the sovereign territory of the East or a coloured portrayal of and distortion of the picture of the Indian society by an 'outsider' in such a way that her fellow countrymen might enjoy and take pride in their own 'superior culture,' but it certainly leaves a bitter taste in the mouth of the Indians, who find this delineation lopsided, prejudiced and commercially-oriented. Understood thus, the novel appears to be a deliberate attempt on the part of the writer to arrest the attention and interest of the readers the world over through her lively and engaging style to have a narcissistic glimpse into the poverty, hunger, filth and garbage that Indian society had been at the time of its writing.

In this way, Jhabvala's major concerns can be summed up in two broad categories—poverty, hunger, filth, exploitation, lust, greed and hypocrisy, metaphorically represented as East, and the sophistication, rootlessness, boredom, gullibility, and material affluence represented as West. And there is a constant clash, cooperation, conflict and compromise between these two extremes running throughout that defines and determines the central thrust of her novels in general and award-winning *Heat and Dust* in particular.

Before discussing the study of narratology with reference to *Heat and Dust*, I'd like to give a brief explanation of the term Narratology. Narratology is the art of narration designed to capture and convey, explore and express the different phases, stages, shades and nuances of the story in terms of realistic details, keen observations and critical comments. So, narratology denotes both the theory and the study of narrative and narratative structure and the ways these affect our perception. While in principle the word may refer to any systematic study of narrative, in practice its usage is rather restricted to narrator and his relationship with other characters and the socio-cultural and economic milieu of the society in the story. Its origin lends to it a strong association with the structuralist's quest for a formal system of useful description applicable to any narrative content.

There are two types of narratives—the homodiegetic narrative and the heterodiegetic narrative. In a homodiegetic narrative, the story is told by a narrator who is also one of story's acting characters—a character on the level of action. For example, the character of Bakha in *Untouchable* is both the narrator and also the part of the story where he captures and expresses the main sequence of events in the book. In a heterodiegetic narrative, the story is told by a narrator who is not present as a character in the story. The fact that a heterodiegetic narrator has a position outside the world of the story makes it easy for us to accept what we would never accept in real life—that somebody should have unlimited knowledge and authority. Heterodiegetic narrators typically assume the power of omniscience—knowing everything, speaking overtly, heterodiegetic narrators can speak directly to their addressees, and they can liberally comment on action, characters, and storytelling itself as it happens in George Eliot. So, it is the tellability of the story that is the focus of this study in which various characters and events, situations and circumstances all together coalesce and contribute to define the central thrust of the novel.

Heat and Dust is a book based on the history of a family envisaging the time span of almost five decades. The narrator of the story herself has reconstructed the story of her step-grandmother Mrs. Olivia Rivers on the basis of a few letters that she has collected from other sources. That means the narrator does not have any primary sources to probe and prove her narration. This form of narratology was prevalent in the eighteenth century when the fiction writers evolved their story from diaries and letters as in Samuel Richardson's *Clarissa*. But Ruth Jhabvala does not allow the readers to have a look at those letters, rather she picks up incidents and details through the narrator's impressions of her reading of those letters and her findings in India as recorded in her diary, and puts them in the shape of an experience, thereby making the narrative a collage of time and space. As the narrator investigates the story, she herself gives birth to a story parallel to the first one—both the stories separated only by time (one taking place in the 1920s and the other in the 1970s).

The art of narration in this novel shifts away from the realistic mode of narration to cinematography as the first part of Olivia's story is told in the third person narrative in the past tense and the second part of the story of the narrator is told in the first person and in the present tense. This shift in time and space allows the novelist not only to telescope the past into the present but also to express and authenticate a view that mechanical division of time is immaterial/irrelevant vis-à-vis basic human nature. That is why, a study in the art of narration becomes all the more imperative and integral both to understand and appreciate the central thrust of the book besides analysing the main concerns of the novelist.

Jhabvala's love-hate relationship with India is dramatically captured in her novel *Heat and Dust* which brought her universal recognition when it won the prestigious Booker Prize in 1975 and was filmed in 1982. The story is told on two planes; the story of Olivia and the story of the narrator. The narrator (who in the film is Anne) tells Olivia's story after visiting Satipur fifty years later. The two separate stories of Anne and Olivia give Jhabvala a chance to portray a double view of Indian society. The image of India as a land of heat and dust both in its physical as well as metaphorical connotations is common in both epochs. Both Olivia and the young protagonist in the latter story share this assessment of the country of their long sojourn. Secondly, there does not seem to be a basic change in the image of the country as it passes from the colonial to the postcolonial India. Shorn of contextual features and incidental details, the basic image of India as a land of exoticism and mystery, of irrational attitudes and devious ways, of spiritual heights and physical degradations continues. In *Heat and Dust*, Ruth continues with another significant feature of her stylistic equipment, that is, irony in order to depict the central thrust of the novel. For instance, in Douglas' spacious house, Olivia gets bored. She has been here for several months and it is only in the evenings or on Sundays that she happens to meet a handful of stereotyped Anglo-Indian officials' families in town. "The rest of the time Olivia was alone in her big house with all the doors and windows shut to keep out the heat and dust. (14).

Similarly, when the Nawab takes Olivia to Baba Firdaus' shrine, they experience terrible heat. "The country they drove: through lay broiling in the sun. . . . At one point the Nawab reached across Olivia to pull down the blind on her window, as if wanting to spare her the sight of all that parched land" (45-46). Both these incidents are replete with a strong irony in the sense that Olivia Rivers gravitates towards the young Nawab to get rid of her loneliness and boredom to the extant that she becomes pregnant. But ignorantly and quite ironically, she is ostracized by her English society and eventually ends up in the mountains all alone. In the same way, the gesture of the Nawab to ward off the sight of the parched and sultry land outside from Olivia is also ironic, because here also the physical scene is symptomatic of the inner psychological and spiritual degeneration in the person of Nawab that will be transferred to her. But the moot question that immediately crops up is whether Jhabvala has given a balanced and unbiased portrayal of this Indian reality and society? To the best of my understanding and belief, the answer to this question is a capital 'NO.' That means she has captured Indian society through her Euro-centric Western spectacles plus a coloured Imperialistic view of her first-hand experiences. Meenakshi Mukherjee hits the nail on its head when she writes: "Jhabvala's failure to develop points to one hazard that the rootless writer is prone to. . . . a result of arrested creative vitality" (91). Even Nissim Ezekiel is not only unhappy with the very title of the book but also finds it a part of a motive attempting to demean India.

In the beginning of the story, the narrator declares that 'this is not my story, it is Olivia's as far as I can follow it. (2) It is as if the narrator is giving a live commentary on the life and living of her grandmother. But quite paradoxically and ironically, she herself becomes the second Olivia. One English couple—a man with his girl friend—after getting bored and disillusioned with England came to India in search of spiritual solace and peace, but to their utter dismay they were robbed, cheated and molested: "To find peace . . . but all I found was dysentery" (21). There is a deliberate use of the method of comparison between the two periods like extra-marital relationship leading to pregnancy, the custom of suttee, hijra-dance etc. Instead of maintaining omniscience, there is the use of only viewpoints, as Jhabvala identifies with two European women and that makes the subject-treatment weak, coloured, biased and lop-sided.

The most pertinent question that remains unattended and also unanswered is whether India is only 'dust, heat, dirt, corruption, cheating and exploitation, or there is something more than what is shown by Jhabvala in the novel. India is certainly a society of rich social and cultural heritage whose past is as glorious as her present is magnificent. Just by showing a few stray incidents in exaggerated and randy idiom, the whole history of India can not be swept under the carpet or simply wished away, because it suits a Western mind for easy popularity and quick success. So, India might be a backward place, a pool of passion, or a place for battle, or even a country of heat, dirt and dust, but it certainly is not the whole reality. The reality of the Indian society envisages the spiritual outpourings of Buddha, the supreme sacrifice and devotion of Savitri and Satyawan, also the path of non-violence and religious tolerance of Mahatma Gandhi, whose contribution in the making of the new world can only be ignored at the peril of one's own critical and complete understanding of India as a torch-bearer and guide to the whole world. Ironically it is the book written and published in independent India, winning the Booker prize, but showing only the half-truths and quarter-lies.

Works Cited

Meenakshi Mukherjee, *The Twice Born Fiction: Themes and Techniques of the Indian Novel in English.* London and New Delhi: Heinemann, 1971.

Ruth Prawer Jhabvala, *Heat and Dust.* London: John Murray, 1975.

Re-Visioning Woman: Towards Spatial Reading Praxis

REKHA BENIWAL

Women-narratives have conventionally been studied as emotional or existential quests. Temporality has generally been privileged as the primary axis in such reading practices. As such, woman's evolution and arrival, her sense of identity and its realization are traced in terms of her temporal representational trajectory. This reading, however, is grossly reductive. It simplifies woman's position in life. Time, no doubt, is an important aspect of woman's 'being' and 'becoming' in this world, but it is not the only element that bears on and impacts her life. Space is an equally important aspect of woman's 'being and becoming' and it works in tandem with time to make a woman what she is. As such, any reading that overlooks the spatial co-ordinate of woman's narrative would only be a gross simplification of woman's story.

This paper attempts to posit an inclusive reading of woman's narrative through an intricate enmeshing of its temporal and spatial co-ordinates. The paper, in fact, tries to demonstrate the relevance of space as a constitutive coordinate of woman's life in society, by undertaking a spatial reading of Ambai's stories. The central argument that this spatial reading is premised on may be summed up as: Woman's position and her roles within society are a function of patriarchal dialectics that invariably revolves around complex and almost hegemonic 'genderisation of space and spatialisation of gender.'

II

Women's writing, at one level at least, can be seen as a redeeming and a recuperating act. This recuperative act, a complex and cumulative interplay of literary and extra-literary processes, manifests itself in contemporary Indian women writing as a discursive potentiality. This not only deconstructs the status-quoist ideological and power-filled seams of patriarchal reality but also reconstructs it by redrawing its gendered map to resurrect woman as a woman per se.

Literary narratives conventionally have been conceived more in terms of events unfolding in a woman's life in time against an inert or empty or indifferent setting. Within this critical tradition 'space/setting' has been treated as "the dead, the fixed, the undialectical, the immobile" and in contrast 'time' has been seen as "rich, fecund, lively and dialectical."[1]

But to view fictional narratives, especially those by women, in terms of conventional temporal-spatial 'active passive hierarchy,' is to miss the complexity or the wholeness of the narrative. The spatial aspect of the narrative is as important and as fecund as the temporal. Space is not a value neutral or passive category.[2] Far from being static entity, spatiality is embedded in the contingency of temporality. Like time, it is a complex and contradictory process, a flux in which human beings continuously intervene. So in order to add complexity to conventional 'feminist' quest criticism, it becomes imperative to approach women's narratives as historical and geographical-spatial entities simultaneously.

The very process of 'writing the woman' entails a critical engagement with patriarchy and, hence gender, both as discursive and substantive category of cultural organisation. As a representational and conceptual category, woman within patriarchy is caught in an ironic ambivalence: on the one hand, she is seen as an essentialised 'being,' a fixed state, and on the other hand, she is constantly manipulated into a 'becoming.' But patriarchy glosses over this ambivalence by positing that both being and becoming are integral aspects of womanhood. Becoming is seen a mere acculturation tool for her notional being. This becoming is rooted through various paths, often violent and torturous, to turn 'woman-as-a-living-entity' into 'woman-as-a-conforming-entity.' Those who conform are idealised, while those who devi-ate or encapsulate tensions and ambiguities, thus producing unstable results, are demonised.

Womanhood, however, is neither fixed by nature, nor it is simply imposed from outside by social norms. Woman as a living entity negotiates her place in gender order by the way she conducts herself in everyday life. She claims, opposes or responds to the place she has been given. The moment one approaches gender this way, the conventional notions of gender get problematised. The notions of dichotomy and difference cast woman into passive receptacles, simplify gender ambiguities (there are masculine women and feminine men), and erase woman as a living entity.[3]

III

The spatial reading praxis helps one transcend the binary conception of gender and see it in a more nuanced manner, in fact as relational power-grids that are complex, contradictory, contextual, arbitrary and unstable.[4] At this point, let me take a story by Ambai,[5] an eminent contemporary Tamil writer, to exemplify what I have been proposing so far.

Ambai in her stories delves into the experience of feminisation as a function of gendered division of physical and social spaces. However, the strategies that she invokes to liberate female and feminine spaces from sexist role patterns, domination and oppression, problematise the patriarchal agenda by suggesting that women belong to but do not solely exist within spatial enclosures. Ambai's stories are generally triggered by a spatial query, "Which is the space we, i.e. women, occupy in life?"[6] She further problematises this fundamental query: "Is it the physical space we inhabit or the space the mind extends to?"[7]

Her stories focus on the vitiation of woman's self and appropriation of allotted space within domestic enclosures. She narrates this aspect of female existence along twin axes—physical and psychological. The physical and the psychological, however, do not form two distinct tools of gendered conditioning, but are seen as interlocking situations that form an uninterrupted continuum, each feeding on and sustaining the other. The story I take here is "A Kitchen in the Corner of the House."[8]

Papaji, the patriarch of the house with a large family—wife, mother, three sons, daughters-in law and grandchildren—live in Ajmer in a Railway compartment like big house. The kitchen, the central metaphor of the story, is situated in the end corner of the house. It's a dark, dingy part of the house where hospitality is a matter of force and pride, where favourite topic of family gatherings is nothing else but food, where food spatialises status, relations and hierarchies. The story is just an extended kitchen, kitchen as physical space, cultural space, psychological space, political space. The story is narrated by Minakshi, one of the three daughters-in-law. Hers is a voice of an outsider as she is outspoken, objective and more importantly not from a Rajasthani culture. She is from idly-dosa culture. The story goes onto narrate the tension between Papaji, the patriarch and Minakshi, the outsider inmate of the family.

Herein the architecture of the house, a concretization of Papaji's patriarchal whims and vision—aptly encapsulates the woman's location/situation within the modern-feudal setting. Within this spatial configuration, the kitchen, though a vehicle for masculine notions of hospitality/honour, is an insignificant utilitarian niche. Ambai's description of the kitchen is very revealing: "Right at the end, the kitchen, stuck on in careless manner" (230). Its spatial arrangement is etched in hues of dark and dank. It parallels woman's position in the household both physically and psychologically. Physically, she is stuck in the kitchen; psychologically the kitchen and the view outside the window personify her reality and desires.

Though insignificant within patriarchal spatiality, "the kitchen in the dark corner" is a locus of power play for the matriarchs of the house: They have so internalised the "set of beliefs" woven around hearth that "the actual details, the concrete facts of kitchen and its space didn't seem to matter to them" (233). Kitchen is where the woman is. There is an incident in the story where the extended family goes for a picnic. The picnic—an excursion into the outer world dependent on masculine patronage—becomes a long preparation/slog in the kitchen. This socio-psycho-spatial conditioning replicates for woman the colonised-coloniser hegemonic arrangement. The kitchen becomes a space for colonised to ingratiate itself in the eyes of the coloniser. The toil of the colonised is a means to boost the luxury of the coloniser. Yet, the little space the coloniser offers to the colonised, becomes a squabbling ground to settle intra-gender rivalry under the false illusion of power. The matriarchs take it to be a pre-ordained destiny, a natural arrangement. The spatial sexism recoils inward on women and leads to intra-gender squabbling as to the control of spaces patriarchy designates to them.

Ambai deconstructs the much-hyped stereotype of 'inside-outside' spaces. She instead posits that even the 'inside' is neither 'autonomous' nor exclusive spatial domain of woman. It is an oppressive spatial arrangement that tends to ghettoise women to the kitchen and sap their identity. She foregrounds this aspect of woman's existence by highlighting the pathetic and inhuman ambience of the kitchen and by deconstructing Jiji-Barijiji's squabbles—the food wars, the control over the keys and kitchen—as a consequence of false consciousness. The control Jiji ultimately exercises over the kitchen and the household has an illusory aura of choice, for the larger decisions are still taken by the patriarch. Instead of conferring authority, this space only encumbers them with responsibility and toil.

Ambai's spatio-temporal critique of the kitchen—embodied through Minakshi –foregrounds it as a de-historicised space, i.e., it is a physical-cultural entity that has been permanently frozen in time. Minakshi's overtures, i.e., her suggestions for renovations in the kitchen, not only disturb the spatial indifference/ equanimity of the patriarch, but also attempt to insert kitchen into history. Minakshi, an outsider-insider in the vein of Sakhi tradition[6], ushers in the importance of female dignity and individuality within the household. This, she argues, can be done through a realignment of gender-space continuum that women are accultured into. This readjustment demands seeing through the constructed-normativity of the spaces and transcending them for larger connections, both with one's inner self and with the world outside.

Ambai thus captures and comprehends the restriction of spatial movement and bodily violence as relatively grosser aspect of patriarchal hegemony. This truism, however, only provides an initial warp and weft for her creative exploration into women's lives. Having located her woman within patriarchal enclosures, she invariably moves on to understand and unearth the psychological and physical contours that such a conditioning/etching subtly imprints on the female self. And in a revelatory final movement, an essential aspect of her story telling technique, she reveals how the physical (space) and the psychological (perception) in women's lives, under the onslaught of patriarchal domination fuse into seamless single reality. And her prescription for action/resistance springs from this realization.

NOTES

1. Michel Foucault, qtd. Wegner, 180, Phillip E. Wegner, "Spatial Criticism: Critical Geography, Space, Place and Textuality," *Introducing Criticism at the 21st Century*, ed. Julian Wolfreys (Edinburgh: Edinburgh UP, 2002) 179-201.
2. Space is "both a production, shaped through a diverse range of social processes and human interventions, and a force that, in turn, influences, directs and delimits possibilities of action and ways of human being in the world" (Wegner).
3. Michel Foucault is another important thinker to highlight the importance of spatial dimension in the evolution of modern civilisation. Visualising it in terms of spatial transformations, he, in his *Discipline and Punish: The Birth of the Prison*, sees spaces as embodiments of power relations wherein everybody finds itself located in a great enclosed, complex, and hierarchical structure and subject to a continuous regime of surveillance and manipulation. He argues that social/ human spaces—homes, prisons, hospitals, and even human bodies—in their present form have been codified through a complex series of power operations, or disciplines—instruments, techniques, procedures, levels of applications, targets—with an aim of producing 'normal' subjects as well as mark-

ing out a whole finely graduated realm of deviances to produce subjected and practised bodies, or "docile" bodies.

4. Connell explains the limitation of these explanatory models thus: A definition in terms of difference means that where we cannot see difference, we cannot see gender. A definition based on dichotomy excludes the patterns of difference among women, and among men, from the concept of gender. A definition in terms of personal characteristics ignores processes which lie beyond the individual person. Large-scale social processes are based on the shared capacities of women and men more than on their differences. Yet the products of the process—the wealth generated, for instance—may be distributed in highly gendered ways.
5. As a writer and a critic, Ambai's (born 1944) literary persona unfolds on two planes: while she carries out her woman-centric creativity under the pseudonym Ambai, she carries out her literary criticism, both in English and Tamil, in her own name, i.e., C.S. Lakshmi. Though a prolific writer in Tamil, till date only two collections exclusively devoted to her short fiction—*A Purple Sea* and *Ambai: Novellas and Essays* that contain Wrestling and Unpublished Manuscript are available in English
6. Gita Krishnankutty, ed., *Ambai: Novellas and Essays* (New Delhi: Katha, 1999) 84.
7. Krishnankutty, 84.
8. Ambai, "A Kitchen in the Corner of the House," *A Purple Sea*, trans. Lakshmi Holmström (2nd ed., Chennai: Manas, 1992).

Home as the Structural Principle in Kiran Desai's *The Inheritance of Loss*

JAGDISH BATRA

Home, it may be argued, is linked to the compulsive primal urge for a safe, exclusive territorial niche to which every living creature aspires. Home means comfort and convenience at the physical level as also at the emotional level, not only because physical condition moulds mental state but also because home points to the presence of family in it. Thus, the emergence of the institution of family added to the importance of home which lies at the intersection of nature and culture. Only a person who does not have home or is far removed from it knows its value. There is no dearth of folk-songs in all cultures that sing of the travails of the *pardesi* or the one who has perforce to stay away from home.

The limits of home expand or contract in different contexts. It could be any territory from the small, walled in space in which one spends most of one's lifetime to the entire country one calls one's 'home country.' This later concept is evoked when one is out of one's own country. Home then, in all its manifestations and interpretations, constitutes the governing principle of the narrative of the Man Booker Prize-winning novel *The Inheritance of Loss* written by Kiran Desai. The title of the novel with its negative overtone, however, refers only to the sense of loss felt by Biju mainly, and by Sai partially towards the end of the novel. The narrative hinges predominantly on the search for home, so much so that it can be called the structural principle of the novel. This is the Tomashevskiian bound motif that is essential to the causal-chronological sequence of the novel. This paper focuses on the concept of home as used in the novel on literal as well as metaphorical planes. An attempt has been made to underline the convergence of concerns regarding the place of origin, security and employment with the structural pattern of the novel.

When we talk about home, habitat forms an integral part of the idea of home. A pleasant environment can make or mar our joyful experience of life. Sensory experience affects the emotional and intellectual life of the people, except of those who have attained perfect dissociation of sensibilities or detached themselves totally from the world. That is why we are concerned about environment. Desai's focus on the geographical nature, apart from being an aesthetic embellishment, also forms an allied motif. To link the narrative script with the underlying concept of home calls for technical ingenuity and a commitment to ecological welfare, both of which Kiran Desai displays in ample measure.

The poem by the Argentinian poet Jorge Luis Borges that serves as the epigraph in *The Inheritance of Loss* states nostalgically: 'My homeland is the rhythm of a guitar, a few portraits, an old sword, the willow grove's visible prayer as evening falls.' He also laments the loss of countryside to the greedy metropolis and of his own inability to 'arrive.' This quite befittingly hints at the theme of the novel. As the narrative begins, we find Sai, the 16-year old luckless daughter of a couple that perished on a Vienna road, approaching, in search of a new home, a decrepit colonial building called Cho Oyu. The house takes its name from a mountain peak on the Nepal-Tibet border and lies twenty kilometers west of the Mount Everest. In Tibetan culture, the term refers to the 'turquoise goddess.' This house denoting loftiness and sublimity is actually located in Kalimpong, a picturesque hill station in the Darjeeling district of West Bengal. The retired judge Jemubhai Popatlal Patel, who presides over this estate, happens to be her maternal grandfather but he is a singular personality in that he jealously guards his privacy. Even though Sai has the judge's blood running in her veins, and has been orphaned through a cruel trick of fate, she is grudgingly allowed by Jemubhai to stay here. The judge had had his education in England. Later, he joined the judicial service in India, then under

British rule. As a result, he had been thoroughly anglicized in etiquette and manners and considered himself a notch higher than others, his close family members included.

Sai's adoption of home, as such, remains incomplete just like her affair with the 20-year old science teacher Gyan, which, if successful, could have made the search for home more meaningful and complete. In this, she arrives at Cho Oyu and yet does not, the lofty peak only beckoning from a distance. She has the company of a cook who tells her stories of spirits and of his son Biju, who is trying to find 'home' in America. His status is that of an illegal immigrant and like thousands of others, he is trying hard to get the green card. *The Inheritance of Loss* is as much the story of Sai as of Biju at the individual level as it is of the Gorkha movement in West Bengal, India, and of the illegal immigrants in the U.S. at the community level. The free run of these parallel narratives is powered by a desire for home until history and politics check them in their tracks with their reactionary and revisionary interpretations.

If the consciousness of home lies at the deeper level in the novel, that of the habitat is felt at the surface level, at the level of allied motif. The idyllic description of the hill station shows Desai's ecological consciousness, which she has inherited from her mother. If Nanda Kaul merges with the atmosphere in *Fire on the Mountain*, in *The Inheritance of Loss*, it is the house that merges with the landscape: 'When she looked back, the house was gone; when she climbed the steps back to the veranda, the garden vanished. [. . .] The gray had permeated inside, as well, settling on the silverware, nosing the corners, turning the mirror in the passageway to cloud' (2). Exotic details of nature—of flora and fauna and lush vegetation—at the foot of the Kanchenjunga presents a veritable feast for the nature lover. Even the solitude of the inhabitants of Cho Oyu has been described in terms of the giant squid spotted there on rare occasions: 'No human had ever seen an adult giant squid alive, and though they had eyes as big as apples to scope the dark of the ocean, theirs was a solitude so profound they might never encounter another of their tribe. The melancholy of this situation washed over Sai'

(2). The house is a crumbling structure in which a 'thousand deceased spiders lay scattered' (12) on the attic floor. A saucer of milk and a pile of sweets is placed by the cook to pacify a pair of black cobras living in a hole. The archetypal cook, as his namelessness suggests, lives in harmony with nature believing that 'The natural world exists in its own right and other beings have a will, a way of their own and their own stories" (Drengson 20).

Sai's parents had also gone to Russia to earn livelihood and to realize a niche, as the environmentalists would say, but unfortunately they met with a fatal accident. That is why Sai, who had been studying in a convent, had to come to her only surviving relative—Jemubhai. In a sense, none of the human beings living at Cho Oyu are the original inhabitants of this place. The building was built by a Scot who left India in 1957. The neighbours include, among others, Lola and Noni, two Anglicized sisters, Uncle Potty, an anglophile from Lucknow and Father Booty, a Swiss national who came here 45 years ago and never thought of going back, satisfied as he was with the pastoral setting in the midst of which he established a dairy. Kalimpong is a fundamental niche or the original home for none of them; each one actually tries to realize the niche.

Sai gets emotionally involved with Gyan, her teacher of Nepalese origin, who lives in the poverty-stricken Bong Busti. Transcending the cultural barriers, nature brings them together. Against the scenic backdrop of the Delo lake or by the shores of the Teesta river, they tell each other tales of themselves and their families. While nature brings them together thus, the cultural politics creates a gulf between the two lovers. The growing discontent among the Indian Nepalese takes the form of the Gorkhaland agitation. Gyan joins this movement and is so much brainwashed that he starts distancing himself from Sai. There is a nasty quarrel between the two and Gyan uses harsh words. He places his geo-ethnic identity above everything else. He berates his beloved and mocks at the 'fake English accent' and 'powdered faces' of 'that fussy pair' at Cho Oyu. He now looks down upon them as encroachers on his homeland.

This mood does not last permanently. When Sai drifts away, he tries to make amends but whether the two are able to unite or not remains an open-ended issue in the novel. Gyan reminisces and feels 'the trouble was that he'd tried to be part of the larger questions, tried to become part of politics and history. Happiness had a smaller location, though this wasn't something to flaunt, of course' (272). Home is also a metaphor for a secure haven. Gyan has realized the difficulties on this path and ended abruptly his honeymoon with the GNLF. His offer to locate the missing Mutt confirms that he is much mellowed later.

The placid life in this beautiful place, disturbed by the unrest among native Nepali community, has its roots in the forcible boundary adjustments done by the erstwhile British rulers and thereafter by our own government on the basis of linguistic organization of states. The GNLF activists, who rob the judge of his old arms, consider the region their original home and therefore want it declared Gorkhaland. When the land belonging to the Bengali sisters is encroached upon by the Gorkha activists, they assert: 'This is our land!' But the Gorkhas would have none of it. (240) While the legitimacy of the hill retreats of people like Justice Jemubhai, Father Booty, Noni and Lola is questioned by the GNLF cadres, their own credentials as inheritors of land might not go beyond a particular point in past, caught up as they are in the 'mythic battles of past vs. present, justice vs. injustice' (295). Even if a group has been here for several generations, the fact remains that it is true so far as the recorded history goes. One cannot make history a ground for claiming a piece of land in these postmodern times when any identity, leave aside the one based on settlement, is fluid and changeable.

II

Trying to realize his own niche is Biju in far-off America, moving from one ill-paid job to the other and also, while working in stuffy kitchens, coming in contact with people from other third world countries—from Pakistan to Zanjibar. He learns that Indians have spread far and wide. They are trying to search for home or realize niches in Guyana, Kenya, Chile, South Africa,

Fiji, New Zealand, Canada etc. He also learns that Indians are discriminated against in many countries from Uganda to Guadeloupe (77). Even in the lottery system that was adopted in the U.S. for granting visas, Indians were not allowed to apply. Ironically, racial prejudices present hurdles in securing home in the world even in postmodern times.

In America, the conditions of work for illegal immigrants are not sound. They live in constant fear of being spotted by the police and are exploited by cheats on the pretext of helping them to get green card. In the severe New York winter, Biju has to put a padding of newspaper under his shirt to keep himself warm. He weeps over his predicament (51). From Baby Bistro to Brigette's, Biju woks in many restaurants before he is finally rendered jobless. In the process, he learns a lot of strategies for survival even as his search for home in the land of plenty remains elusive.

In that pitiable condition, nostalgia for home overtakes him so strongly that in his imagination, he can smell the humid air of Kalimpong and hear the sound of silver grass. Finally, he decides to return to India. As ill luck would have it, he is robbed of everything by the Gorkhaland militants before he lands at Cho Oyu and meets his father. But for him, the loss is still worth inheriting, because he has finally reached back home. What is important for him is not the material loss but the gain of home. Clearly, the title of the novel *The Inheritance of Loss* does not convey the emotive truth.

The talk about home will not be complete if its macro form—the home-country—is not discussed. International politics enters this discourse about home through the backdoor. Kiran Desai makes her characters talk about colonialism which was, simply put, all about divesting the native people of their home. The owners of the Brigette's restaurant are shown reading the *New York Times* report which mentioned how the third world people, the 'former slaves and natives' of the myriad newly decolonized nations, came to America 'screaming colonialism, screaming slavery, screaming mining companies screaming banana companies oil companies screaming CIA spy among the missionaries' (134). That in effect means the colonized are aware of the machinations of the powerful in the world to capture their home country's politics and economy through economic imperialism. People like Achootan want green card as a matter of right with the logic which he had developed in England: 'Your father came to *my* country and took *my* bread and now I have come to *your* country to get *my* bread back' (135). This is raw logic but surely it has a lot of sense in it.

Kiran Desai examines the construct of home inside out. What about the exploitation of Indians by Indians in America? Do the exploiters forget their common home (shared niche), after they have 'realized' niche in the U.S.A.? When Biju slipped on some rotten spinach in the kitchen of Gandhi Café, the owner Harish-Harry refused to call in a doctor, because according to him, it was Biju's responsibility to keep the floor clean. Again, when the compensation for lost baggage is being doled out at the Calcutta airport, only to the NRIs and not to Indians, the former could afford to maintain a cool posture, looking thoroughly civilized while the latter, having lost greenbacks, raise a hue and cry. (298) So, being civilized, which is a cultural phenomenon as against natural, is tied to simple selfishness.

While the concept of home is in consonance with nature and every creature craves for one, human culture politicizes it. We can lay claim to a place as our original, ancestral, ethnic or racial home at the cost of historical knowledge only. Man tends to interpret motives of purity of race or lay claim to a piece of land to suit his existential needs only. The nature-man relationship has ever been problematized as Desai's remark towards the close of the novel suggests it without assigning any value to it but, all the same, giving it a biocentric focus: "All night it would rain. It would continue, off and on, on and off, with savagery [. . .] the town would slide down the hill. Slowly, painstakingly, like ants, men would make their paths and civilization and their wars once again, only to have it wash away again" (323). Surely, the quest for home as a manifestation of the existential aspirations of man would not be thwarted merely because of this tussle between nature and culture. Leonard Lutwack's observation about the earth could fittingly sum up this submission: "It is a hostile, alien place; and yet also man's true home" (Qtd. Howarth 86).

Works Cited

Desai, Anita. *Fire on the Mountain*. London: William Heinemann, 1977.

Desai, Kiran. *The Inheritance of Loss*. New Delhi: Penguin, 2006.

Drengson, Alan. 'Novels, Philosophical Studies and Ecocriticism' *Indian Journal of Ecocriticism*. Aug. 2009.

Howarth, William. 'Some Principles of Ecocriticism.' *The Ecocriticism Reader*, ed. Cheryl Glotfelty & Harold Fromm. Athens: The University of Georgia, 1996.

The Prose Style and Narrative Technique in the Fiction of Mulk Raj Anand

JYOTI SHEORAN

Style is one of those literary terms which is promiscuously used, but cannot be satisfactorily defined. It may mean too little or too much. It may signify approbation or derogation. The word style includes the thing done, as well as the manner of doing it. The dictionary meanings of style include: manner of writing, speaking, or doing, collective characteristics of the writing or diction or artistic expression proper to a person or school or period or subject; and noticeably superior quality or manner. In a technical way, the ancient meaning of style is "a writing instrument, a small rod with pointed end for scratching letters on wax-covered tablets and blunt end for obliterating" as Anand wrote in a letter to Saros Cowasjee. Buffon had made his celebrated remark "Style is the man." Socrates had said, "As a man is, so is his speech." As per Gibbons "Style is the image of character." Schopenhauer has said, "Style is the physiognomy of the mind," while Longinus believes that "elevation of style is the echo of a great soul." All these are affirmations of Buffon's thought.

The present paper attempts to highlight the stylistic and narrative techniques in the novels of Mulk Raj Anand. The style or selection of words, characters, scenes, situation and way of presenting the message that the author communicates to the reader, along with how the author chooses to present it, produce an author's individual style, which, given the quirks and vagaries of human personality, necessarily varies from author to author.

Anand's use of slang, swear words, jargon of abuse, epithets of low-life, and verbal coinages takes him nearer his avowed purpose of evolving a language as rich and powerful as Irish English. However, the intrusion of the unpoetical, the slangy, and the coarse appears mostly in the dialogue. The narrative nearly always moves in conventional, exalted, and purposive prose. A Conrad or a Nabokov writing in an alien language has replenished the beauty of that language. In India, Anand has rejuvenated the English language through innovations, borrowings, and other sources of enrichment. He has created a language which has a rough rhythm of its own as well as a normal calm central to good style; and rhythm and calmness co-exist for the sake of relevance. He violently mixes the idiosyncrasies of Punjabi with the urbanity of English speech. The result is flashy "fireworks," in which language is chastened and renewed.

Anand's pen is neither delicate enough nor his touch too sure. His 'naturalistic' prose, with loads of swear words and expressions, literally translated from the vernacular idiom, often produces a crude and ludicrous effect. The reader is prone to be offended at the indelicate, and at times unmeaning, oaths which proceed from the mouths of some of his characters. Usually the profanities and swear-terms appear in the original native form, as for example, "gandu," "bitichod" and "sala."

Sometimes, he renders such expressions literally into English: "May they die," "rape daughter," "rape sister," "son of a donkey by a mule," "seed of an owl" etc. Such abuses and slang terms make his style literal, artificial, floundering and poor; and perhaps a bit shocking also. Commonplace Hindustani words and a literal rendering of proverbs and idiomatic phrases further hinders Anand's style from penetrating the idea like a dagger-thrust. Such Indianization and literal transcriptions are the rule and not the exception: "No one can enter a little door seated on a camel," "lands not ploughed in May, cattle not grass fed in August and girls pampered in their parents houses—these three are always ruined," " a camel to ride and a cock to eat," "find sand in the butter," "friends-since-the days-when-they-wore-napkins-in-their-cradles," "mooch," "Khichri," "Jungle pani," "mahurat," "asirvad," "izzat," "hai hai," "chamar."

Bastard English derivatives are not infrequent either. To name but a few, we find "Daktar," "Sire," "Notus." "Cirgutus," "Magister," "Injans," "Kernal Sahib," "Motur Cars," "Wulcome," "Lafterns," "Mistha," "Diputy Collacter," "Gold flik," "Policia,." Only in *Untouchable* did Anand take the trouble of using italics for the Hindustani words inserted.

If the creation of a novelist is to reach technical excellence, the plot and temporal rhythm of the imagined world and the order of presentation should be cleverly interspersed. Sudden and unaccounted shifts, twists and arbitrary ends to a situation make the readers feel removed in time and space from the fictional world. It is only occasionally that Anand over-emphasises the device of coincidence. But in *Coolie* he abuses chance as crudely as is common in a thriller or a melodrama. The accidents are not only inseparable from the passions and actions of the character but also somewhat inconsistent with the entire design. Contrivance is used to provide surprises, to keep the action moving somehow and even to produce an unhappy ending. In fact, chance helps forge the chain of events in this novel.

It is the chance meeting of Munoo with Ganpat and Prabha that results in a comparatively comfortable existence for the hero in Daulatpur. In the person of the elephant driver - another chance acquaintance, Munoo finds a friend who takes him to Bombay. In Bombay, soon after his arrival, the protagonist chances to save a poor girl and her poor parents, who get him a job and offer him board and lodging by way of gratitude. It is a car accident that helps the novelist to take this ill-starred character of his to the Shimla Hills and incidentally, to an early grave. Then there is an accident (both literal and figurative) in *Two Leaves and a Bud* that cuts down Gangu (a character getting a little cumbersome) and rounds off a narrative that had almost run its course. Anand is here too actively associated with the doings of his characters.

Anand borrows from the social history, but usually fails to separate himself from the material. He rarely discovers and defines the meaning of his subject matter as did, say Defoe in *Moll Flanders*. He stands away from all new fangled novel designs. In technique, he is a traditionalist and not an experimentalist. With him, there is no sensitive arrangement of events. His approach is historical- a mechanical reconstruction or recapitulation of the 'past.' He does not ordinarily follow the technique which Ford Madox Ford and Joseph Conrad called 'the chronological looping method' and more commonly known as the 'time-shift' technique. Nowhere do we find in him the closed plot based on causality or the double plot based on back-and-forth alteration in time. An impressionist, who is aware of the effect of a scene rather than of the scene itself, Anand feels his way tentatively, adding fact to fact. The effect of the generalized picture supporting the play of action makes it a kind of propulsivẽ force.

As Anand's technique is based on a single sequence which was so popular with writers of picaresque fiction, the transition of his characters through time is unlike a wave increasing and swelling every instant, but bears a close similarity to regular progression along a line. He takes notes from life and logically classifies them under the head of the biography of character. Consequently, the shape of his books is the shape of protagonist's existence. *Untouchable* is a page from Bakha's life and *The Road* from Bhikhu's. *The Village* trilogy deals with a big chunk from Lal Singh's career and the *Two Leaves and a Bud* from Gangu's. *The Big Heart* depicts significant events in Ananta's life, *Coolie* in Munoo's and *Death of a Hero* in Maqbool Sherwani's.

In each one of these novel, is piled a series of episodes deriving a sort of unity from the personality of the central character. Rarely is an attempt made to plumb the deeper levels of human nature—the fore-conscious and the sub-conscious—the depths where experience and awareness proceed not entirely or mainly in verbal medium, but are tactile and mobile, visional and aural too. Occasionally he peels, like Peter Cynt, the wild onion in his search for the kernel, the germ of life, but stops much short of psychological fiction wherein the structure of the novel liquifies into a ceaseless stream of events, set in a ceaseless stream of commentary.

Time with Anand is chronological-time, by clock and calendar. It is conceptual but not psychological and is rarely, if ever, by the hero's or heroine's private watch; and the running of sand is hardly ever measured by value and intensity. In *Untouchable*, he describes a day's events, from morning to evening, in the life of Bakha. In his second novel *Coolie* he depicts the life of a 'hill-boy' a span extending from early childhood to adolescence. In *The Village*, *Across the Black Waters* and *The Sword and the Sickle*, Lal Singh's story is sketched upto a turbulent middle age covering his childhood, adolescence and youth. *The Old Woman and the Cow* opens with Gauri's marriage and completes just before her period of gestation. *The Seven Summers* is distilled from seven years and *Death of a Hero* takes a little less than seventy-two hours to work out. Only in *The Road* and *Private Life of an Indian Prince* is 'time' a bit vague, if not indefinite. In *The Big Heart*, it is a character in its own right—pulsating, visible and audible. The action is encompassed within the last day of Ananta on this earth which begins at 5:00 a.m. and is over by 7:30 p.m. The clock tower in the city of Amritsar, whose chimes punctuate Ananta's unwary but definite march towards the grave, directly impounds the environment. It sounds its presence at each important turn and juncture of the plot as sketched in the novel. As the description on the very first page of *The Road* goes, it is a:

> Monument which ushered in the iron age, with the fancy weather-lock on its steep needle, which talks to the sky and records the evanescent moods of the winds and the spheres, and with its gigantic four-faced English clock from which the families with two or three storeyed houses in Billimaran can read the movement of the two hands of the new God, Time.

Instead of overlapping the gaps between one action and the next, Anand prefers to achieve a smoother effect of continuity by severely restricting the fictional time. The enlargement of the dramatic and the passing over of the ordinary by means of foreshortening and concentration of telescoping, produce a closeness of texture that is artistically satisfying - a clear and close narrative. But in a way, these also provide an intolerable deal of sag. The heterogeneity and the irrelevance of life are carefully eliminated in accordance with the principle of artistic economy. But when he ventures to render a substantial length of time as in *The Village* trilogy and in *Seven Summers*, the material is so scanty (and neither positive nor concrete) that the composition as a consequence gets threadbare.

The particular account and stir of life, the life behind the story is always interesting. Anand seems to look for it most readily, not so much in the nature of men and women whose action makes this story but in the streets and factories and houses. He cannot think of his people without the home they inhabit. With him, to imagine a human being is to imagine a province, a village, a corner of a slum, a turn of the street, or market place. Exhaustive particulars are made known and nothing of the local colour is excluded lest the action be damaged: A survey of the thathiar 'mohalla' in the city of Amritsar reads:

> Dating from the 'age of truth,' there are about thirty to forty of these houses, large and small. The large ones are mainly the tall ones, belonging to the few well-to-do coppersmith families who, rising from humble beginning, have prospered in the 'iron age' and built one storey on top of another, gradually, on the fourteen to twenty-yards square of earth on which their old hovels stood. The small ones, inhabited by the bulk of coppersmith community of Amritsar jut out of each other in curious shapeless tangles. They show the architecture, specially for the craftsman, called *thathiars* . . . was not the strong point of the 'age of truth' or may be, this lane was the particular hell to which the coppersmith families were consigned by *Karma* or Destiny because someone in the community once killed a cat, which is why the lane is called Ballimaran, Cat Killer's lane, but crumbling and rickety, the hovels rest on the firm foundations of the earth beneath them. (Buhler, *The Laws of Manu*, Oxford, 1886, 301-2)

Anand adopts the technique of stream-of-consciousness novels like Joyce's *Ulysses* in so far as he presents the thought-currents of Bakha created by the moment of pollution. But, as in stream-of-consciousness novel, here the plot is not cracking and the story element has not disappeared. *Untouchable* has a metamorphosis of technique and content. The plot is well-knit, compact and organic. The perfect plot occurs when there is a causal connection between character and situation. In *Untouchable*, the plot grows out of the interplay of Bakha's character and circumstances. There are no loose ends about the story and the plot is not rambling, stagy or theatrical, simply because it is compact and brief. Though the novel moves slowly, it has too much stuff packed in it and this, in turn, has given tightness to the plot. After analysing the novel, C.D. Narasimhaiah eulogizes this quality of compactness and shortness: "And that all this experience should have been packed with the intensity of the poetic into a short span of twenty-four hours is a remarkable triumph of the technique; the full implications of its application to this novel being hardly realized by those who glibly comment on its 'stream-of-consciousness technique' as though that were in itself a merit of the book."

Style and Plot Structure in R.K. Narayan's Novels

ANITA DALAL

R.K. Narayan contributed a series of novels over many decades and continued writing till his death. He had a long and deep association with Graham Greene who helped him find a publisher in England. He is one of the most artistic of Indian writers, who aim at providing aesthetic pleasure. This paper offers a probe into such stylistic features of Narayan's fiction as the art of narration, plot-structure, use of mythical technique, Indianness, characterization, use of wit, irony and humour, choice of diction and range of vocabulary.

R.K. Narayan is pre-eminently a story-teller. Like a traditional story teller, he writes with a natural flow. He has words coming easily and effortlessly leading to the loosely structured form of fiction. Narayan—not a "master of wider vocabulary" (Parameswaran 56), uses a language which invariably possesses a deceptive simplicity. In his fiction, there is a conspicuous recurrence of the process of one's self-realization through a network of social, political and cultural institutions and practices. He focuses on the character and action, but only within the framework of the story of the novels. The plots of his novels are thin, loose, episodic and lacking in the unity of action.

Most of his novels are straightforward narrations in which he records the events as they occur without bothering much about the consistence or coherence of plot-structure and other formal elements of the art. Plot and character are interwoven in such a way that character proves to be the determinant of action which in turn establishes the features of the character. In *The Man Eater of Malgudi*, Nataraj and Vasu—the taxidermist, meet and the tension between them grows instantly. The story is narrated in the first person by Nataraj, the printer. In chapter I, there is an account of Nataraj's family, friends and that of his occupation. In Chapter II, we are introduced to Vasu, who takes possession of Nataraj's attic and converts it into nothing less than a charnel house. Subsequently, complications arise as the attic starts emitting foul smell of dead animals. To add to the complexity, Vasu brings a law suit against Nataraj. When Vasu is prevented from shooting, he turns to womanising. Later, he plans to shoot the temple elephant. However, he himself dies in mysterious circumstances. This mystery is somehow cleared in the end by Sastri who reveals that the evil destroyed itself like the demon Bhasmasura.

In Narayan's realism, everything is inter-related in the sense that there is a composite of scenes, characters and events representing life as a whole. Consider the following excerpt from *The Financial Expert*:

> Margayya's blood was completely the city man's and revelled in crowds, noise and bustle; the moment he looked out and saw the stream of people and traffic flowing up and down the road, he felt that he was in the right place. A poet would perhaps have felt exasperated by the continuous din, but to Margayya, it was like background music to his own thoughts. There was a row of offices and shops opposite, insurance agencies, local representatives of newspapers, hair-cutting saloons, some film distributors, a lawyer's chamber, and hardware shop, into which hundreds of people were going everyday. (110)

In the narrative, Narayan also comments on the meaning of the protagonist's name: "Marg" means the way and "Ayya" is a suffix to it. Margayya means one who shows the way. Here the protagonist shows the way to the poor peasants to draw huge loans from the co-operative bank, without committing themselves to repay the same. The use of the word "money" is conspicuously repetitive. However, the ending of the narrative ironically places Margayya in the beginning.

The Vendor of Sweets and *The Financial Expert* have almost similar pattern of the development of the plots. In both these works, the narration proceeds from a single point of view. Both the heroes, Jagan and Margayya are inclined towards attaining wealth in their lives, however Jagan is an improvement over Margayya in the sense that "he appears to be very cultivated, has faith and sympathy, and maintains happy relationship with his servants, businessmen, and friends" (Prasad 76).

From Narayan's other novels, *The Guide* deviates in certain significant aspects. Unlike the straightforward narrations in most of the novels, the plot of *The Guide* is comparatively more complex than those of other works. This novel manifests a complexity and multiplicity of meanings. The most important of this "Complex of meanings is the self and the roles it can play" (Prasad 92). First of all, Raju plays the role of a tourist guide to a particular family, then he assists Marco in completing a scholarly work. He also motivates Rosie to realize her potential as an artist. Later, he plays the role of a spiritual guide to a community. However, he hardly remains successful in realizing his identity in any of the diverse roles played by him. In the first six sections, we have the narrator and Raju alternately narrating, so that the "narrative voice may be taken as a chorus that specifies the scope of what Raju has to say about himself and his activities" (Prasad 87). Sections seven, eight, nine and ten constitute Raju's confession of his past experiences. The concluding section portrays Raju's efforts to live the life of a saint.

Similar to Thomas Hardy's Wessex, Narayan created, for the settings of his novels, the fictitious town of Malgudi manifesting the representative traits of Indian experience. Malgudi is Narayan's "imaginary locale like the 'Lake District' of Wordsworth, 'border countries' of Sir Walter Scott, 'The Wessex' of Thomas Hardy and 'the Five Towns' of Arnold Bennet" (Singh 47). Various researchers and critics have attempted to identify the original Malgudi as K.R.S. Iyengar says, "Can it be that Lalgudi, in the Trichinopoly District, and fringing the river Cauvery, is the original of Malgudi?" Narayan's novels emphasize the settings, customs, dress, speech, dialect and social set-up of Malgudi not merely as local colour, but as the conditions affecting the ways of thinking, feeling and behaviour of the characters. He stresses the general human issues and characteristics which can be traced anywhere in the world.

The inhabitants of Malgudi, though possessing certain individualistic traits, are essentially human. Malgudi is a symbol of a typically South-Indian town which, with each new novel, gradually grows in size and importance. It grows from a small town or village in *Swami and Friends* to a big city in *The Vendor of Sweets*. Narayan has rendered a good synthesis of the old and the new. Even in the early thirties, Malgudi had a Municipality, a Town hall, a club and two new schools. Even in *Swami and Friends*, one can witness motor cars and clubs as Swami enjoys a thrilling ride to the club in the car of his father's friend. Narayan's Malgudi in 1935 gets more or less modernized as 'Palace Talkies,' a well-equipped theatre, substitutes the old, sheet-roofed 'Variety Hall,' which for ages had entertained the citizens of Malgudi with silent films. The other new landmarks include the Engladia Insurance Company, The Regal Hair-cutting Saloon, the Malgudi Photo-Bureau, the suburban stores and co-operative banks etc. Undoubtedly, the spirit of the place influences character and action. The ruined temple, the flowing Sarayu and the stone slab influence Raju in *The Guide*, and help him to face the final ordeal of the fast and also contribute to his sainthood.

Another distinctive feature of Narayan's works is the use of mythical technique. He is well versed in the Hindu epics, like the *Ramayana* and the *Mahabharata* and Hindu scriptures, myths and legends which form a part of the Indian folklore. This is clearly brought out by a study of his work entitled *Gods, Demons and Other Stories*, which abounds in references and allusions to myths and legends. In this way, Narayan tries to render the variety and chaotic complexity of modern life. In a remarkably successful way, the writer has used the Bhasmasura myth in *The Man Eater of Malgudi*. In this novels, Vasu is evil incarnate as he frightens children, kills dogs, repels neighbours with the stretch of his workshop and defies social conventions by bringing in prostitutes. The use of Bhasmasura myth stresses the self-destructive nature of Vasu. Sastri, drawing upon different myths, comments on the lives of various demons to prove his point:

> There was Ravana, the protagonist in the *Ramayana*, who had ten heads and twenty arms. . . . The earth shook under his tyranny. Still he came to a sad end. Or take Mahisha, the *asura*, who had secured an especial favour that every drop of blood shed from his body should give rise to another demon in his own image and strength, and who nevertheless was destroyed. The Goddess with six arms, each bearing a different weapon, came riding for the fight on a lion which sucked every drop of blood drawn from the demon. Then there was Bhasmasura, who acquired a special boon that everything he touched should be scorched, while nothing could ever destroy him. God Vishnu was incarnated as a dancer of great beauty, named Mohini. She promised to yield to him only if he imitated all the gestures. At one point in the dance, Mohini placed her palms on her head, and the demon followed this gesture in complete forgetfulness and was reduced to ashes. Everyman can think that he is great and will live forever, but no one can guess from which quarter his doom will come. (54)

His novels manifesting this faith in the victory of the good over the evil forces, the different concepts of Indian philosophy, Indian traditions and customs constitute a conspicuous Indianness. "Narayan is a traditionalist and his novels are the mirrors of the Hindu customs and traditions adhered to by the overwhelming majority of Indians. He vests most of his characters in his writings in a traditional garb" (Girija 27). The stress on the role of the family is clearly witnessed in *The Bachelor of Arts* and the typical housewife bearing the tyranny of her husband is reflected in the image of Savitri in *The Dark Room*. In *The Guide*, Rosie's solicitude for her husband and the attitude of resignation she adopts when Raju is arrested for forgery displays her Indianness. The exploitation of many popular superstitions, rituals and beliefs, the use of such motifs as cobras and dancing girls, the introduction of such characters as 'sadhus,' 'sanyasis,' and 'swamis' are also steps in the same direction. In *The Guide* Rosie reads *Natya Shastra* of Bharat Muni and dances like a cobra to the music of a flute. However, in one aspect, R.K. Narayan departs from the Indian tradition. He makes no attempt to preach in his works and thus steers clear of didacticism. He neither tries to be judgmental nor does he impose his views on the readers.

Narayan—the greatest of the humorists among the Indian English novelists—uses variety of humour: humour of character, humour of situation and verbal humour arising from jokes, jests, retorts and repartees. Most of the time, his humour is gentle, genial and kindly. He satirises the greedy money lenders, black marketeers, fake *sadhus* and naive characters. In *Swami and Friends* and *The Bachelor of Arts*, the deflation of the image of a teacher and that of a professor is highly humorous. Narayan also uses his subtle sense of humour in the delineation of such minor characters as the landlord in *The English Teacher*, the Madras rake in *The Bachelor of Arts* and the peculiar priest in *The Financial Expert*.

In *The Man Eater of Malgudi*, Narayan's use of humour of character is focussed on the constant discomfiture of Nataraj. He seems nothing more than a passive spectator as Vasu takes possession of his attic and treats his parlour as the extension of the attic. Vasu bullies Nataraj and his friends while Nataraj's attempts at self-assertion always remain futile. One cannot help laughing when Nataraj is carried away by Vasu in his jeep without a single penny in Nataraj's pocket, without buttons to his shirt but with his fears at the rash and reckless driving of Vasu. In certain cases, humour also arises from the way in which actions, people and their motives are described by the novelist. Consider the following excerpt from *The Man Eater of Malgudi*:

> The matter with me was that I was not able to say 'no' to anyone and that got me into complications with everyone, from a temple prostitute to a taxidermist. I repeated to myself all the stinging rejoinders I should have hurled at my wife. . . . So, when my wife asked, 'What is your business with her?' I should have instantly said, 'I want to seduce Rangi or be seduced by her.' If my wife had said, 'of all women,' I should have replied, 'Yes, of course, you are blinded by jealousy. No doubt she chews tobacco and looks rugged but she has it, it comes through even when she whispers to you. How can any man resist her. (116)

The ironic and satiric humour is seen in Narayan's exposure of the ways in which the lawyer fleeces his clients, the ways and greed of the bus-conductors, police inspectors, and astrologers. Thus, he uses the humour of character, of situation and of verbal humour. However, it is "difficult to placė Narayan's comedy in any one of the well known categories like the comedy of manners, the problem comedy, the dark comedy, or the farcical and the satirical. In most fictions of Narayan, all these comic strains are noticeable, but none of them constitutes the dominant mode" (Prasad 100).

Though the writing style of R.K. Narayan suffers from certain shortcomings such as the violation of the unity of action, lack of synthesis of realism and fantasy, limited canvas of characters, limited vocabulary; yet his simple and lucid style, genial humour, natural expressions, portrayal of true Indian philosophy surpass many writers and establish him as one of the most prominent Indians writing in English. The Scottish thinker Alexander McCall Smith avers, "Narayan's insight, biographical writing style and deeply humane humour not only influenced me as a writer, but also gave me immense pleasure as a reader"

Works Cited

Girija, S. "Indian Customs and Conventions Depicted in the Writings of R.K. Narayan." *Indian Writings in English*. Ed. Manmohan K. Bhatnagar and M. Rajeshwar. Vol. 7. New Delhi: Atlantic, 2000.

Iyengar, K.R.S. *Indian Writing in English*. Calcutta: Asia, 1973.

Narayan, R.K. *The Man-Eater of Malgudi*. New Delhi: Penguin, 1983.

___. *The Man-Eater of Malgudi*. New Delhi: Penguin, 1983.

___. *The Financial Expert*. Mysore: Indian Thought Publications, 1967.

Parameswaran, Uma. *A Study of Representative Indo-English Novelists*. New Delhi: Vikas, 1976.

Prasad, V.V.N. Rajendra. *Five Indian Novelists*. New Delhi: Prestige, 1990.

Singh, Pramod Kumar. *Major Indo-English Novelists and Novels*. Jaipur: Sublime, 2001.

Smith, Alexander McCall. "R. K. Narayan is one of my greatest inspirations: Scottish author." Nov. 2009. <http://www.twocircles.net/2009jan30/Scottish_author.html>.